MENSA

VISUAL
BRAINTEASERS

Editor: Tim Dedopulos
Senior Art Editor: Zoe Maggs
Design: Pauline Hoyle
Production: Garry Lewis

Printed in Great Britain

MENSA

VISUAL
BRAINTEASERS

John Bremner

CARLTON

Contents

AMERICAN MENSA LIMITED

American Mensa Ltd is an organization for people who have one common trait: an IQ in the top 2% of the nation. Over 50,000 current members have found out how smart they are. This leaves room for an additional 4.5 million members in America alone. You may be one of them.

If you enjoy mental exercise, you'll find lots of good "workout programs" in the *Mensa Bulletin*, our national magazine. Voice your opinion in one of the newsletters published by each of our 150 local chapters. Learn from the many books and publications that are available to you as a member.

Are you a "people person," or would you like to meet other people with whom you feel comfortable? Then come to our local meetings, parties, and get-togethers. Participate in our lectures and debates. Attend our regional events and national gatherings. There's something happening on the Mensa calendar almost daily. So, you have lots of opportunities to meet people, exchange ideas, and make interesting new friends. Maybe you're looking for others who share your special interest? Whether yours is as common as crossword puzzles or as esoteric as Egyptology, there's a Mensa Special Interest Group (SIG) for it.

Take the challenge. Find out how smart you really are. Contact American Mensa Ltd today and ask for a free brochure. We enjoy adding new members and ideas to our high-IQ organization.

American Mensa Ltd,
1229 Corporate Drive West,
Arlington, TX 76006-6103.

Or, if you don't live in the USA and you'd like more details, you can contact Mensa International, 15 The Ivories, 628 Northampton Street, London N1 2NY, England, who will be happy to put you in touch with your own national Mensa.

THE
PUZZLES

Draw three straight lines that will give you six sections with 1 clock, 2 hares and 3 lightning bolts in each section.

1

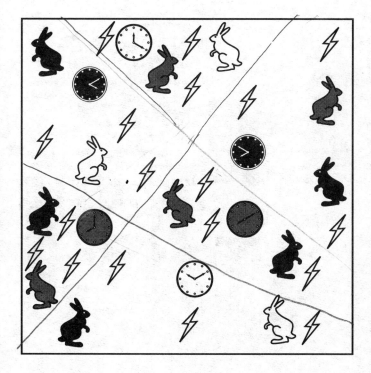

see answer 11

This figure is a collection of blocks rotated through four perspectives. How many blocks are there in total?

208 blocks

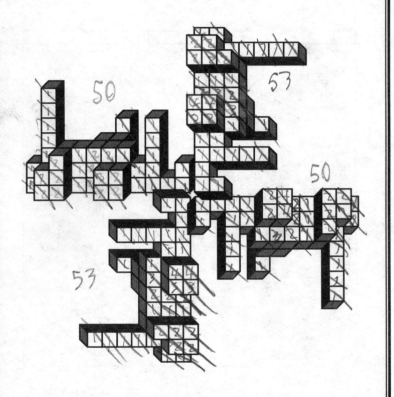

50

53

50

53

see answer 32

Which two of these butterflies are identical?

A

B

C

D

E

F

see answer 53

Which of the following is the odd one out?

B is odd

A

B

C

D

see answer 75

Which panel goes in the gap?

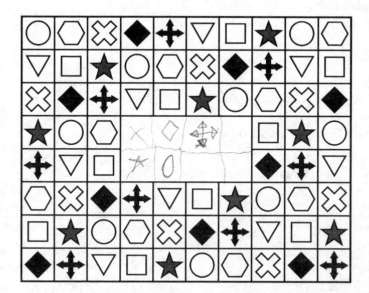

A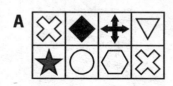

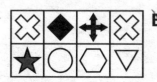 **B**

C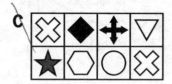

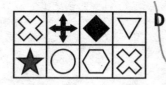 **D**

see answer 97

Which of the following is the odd one out?

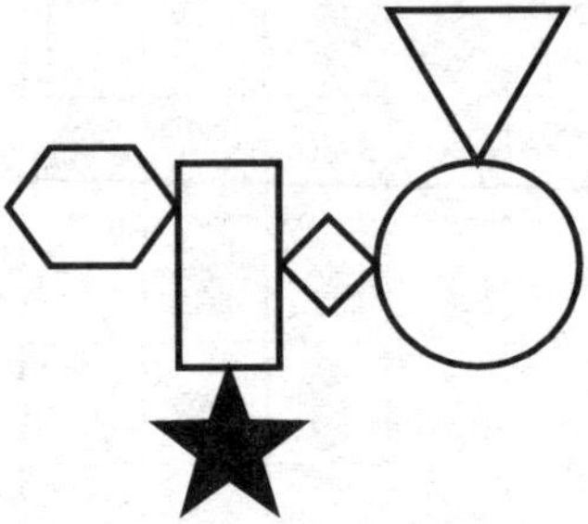

A

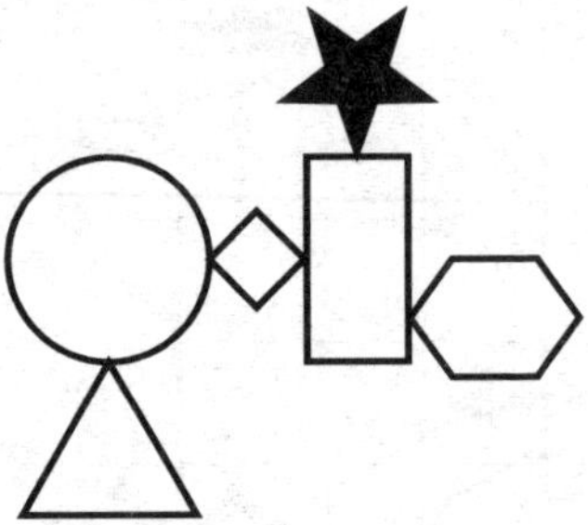

B

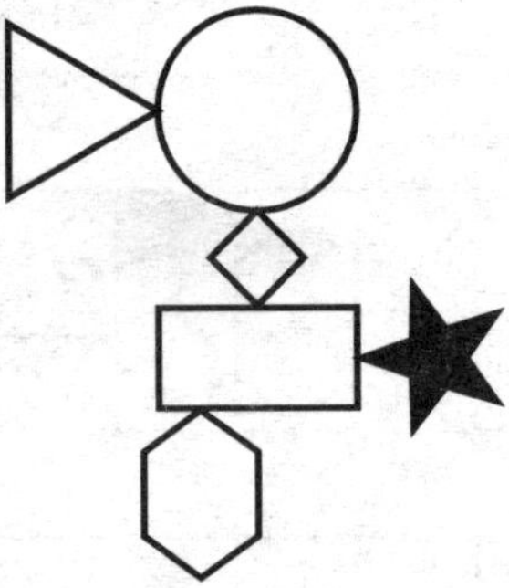

C

D

see answer 119

Which of the following penguins is the odd one out?

A

B

C

D

see answer 141

Complete the analogy.

 is to

as **DIRT** is to ?

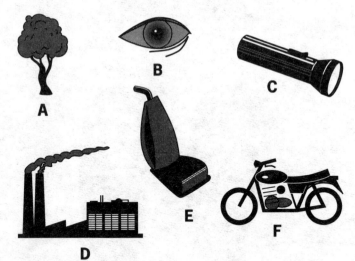

A

B

C

D

E

F

see answer 162

Which of the following is the odd one out?

B is odd

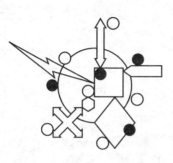

A

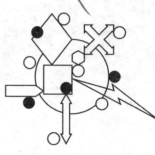

B

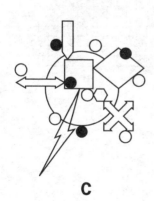

C

D

see answer 152

How many black spotted tiles are missing from this design?

14

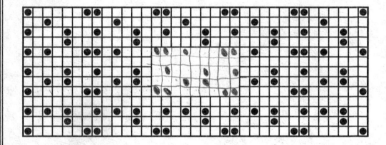

see answer 130

If the black arrow pulls in the direction indicated, will the load rise or fall?

rise

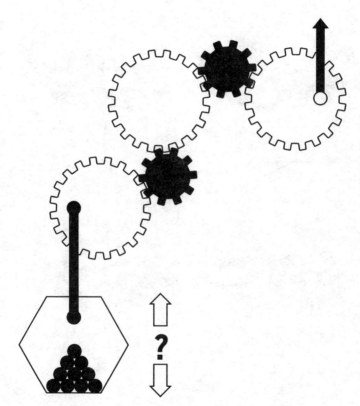

see answer 108

B+C

see answer 86

When old gardener Lincoln died, he left his grandchildren **13**
19 rose bushes each. The grandchildren, Agnes (A), Billy
(B), Catriona (C) and Derek (D), hated each other, and so
decided to fence off their plots as shown. Who had to build
the greatest run of fence?

Billy

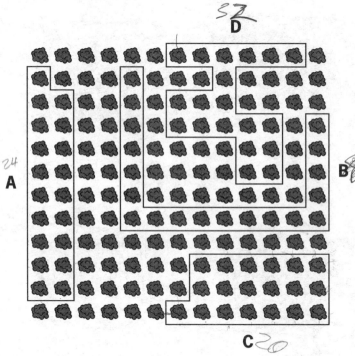

see answer 64

23

14 Which of these spiders and their webs make two identical pairs?

$$\frac{A+B}{C+D}$$

A

B

C

D

see answer 43

A is odd

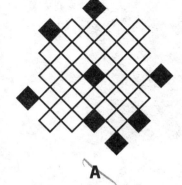

A

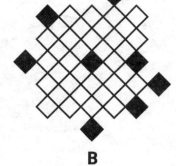

B

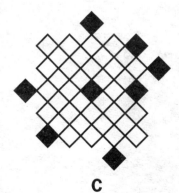

C

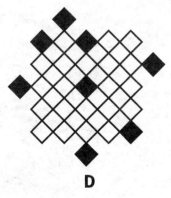

D

see answer 22

16 Spot the 10 differences in picture B.

A

1. flag color (small)
2. person w/big flag's tongue
3. had band
4. hole in tooth gone
5. man with sun
6. Glasses white
7. color of shirt
8.
9.
10.

B

see answer 1

Shade in this map of the USA Midwest using no more than 4 tints, so that no adjacent borders have the same hue.

see answer 12

Which of the following is the odd one out?

A is odd.

A

B

C

D

see answer 33

28

C is odd.

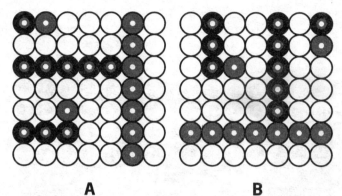

A   **B**

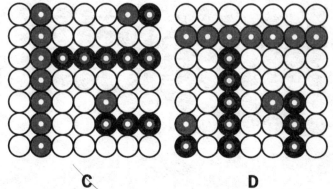

C   **D**

see answer 54

How many bricks are missing from this wall?

see answer 76

B+C are the same, but so are A+D

B+C are diff. from A+D

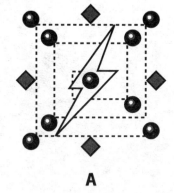

A

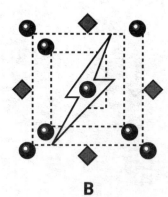

B

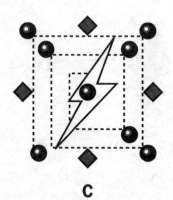

C

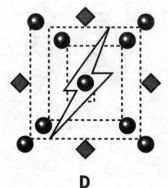

D

see answer 98

Which shape should replace the question mark, A, B, C, or D?

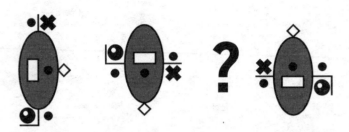

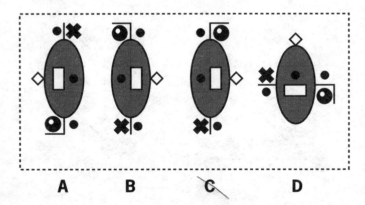

A   **B**   **C**   **D**

see answer 120

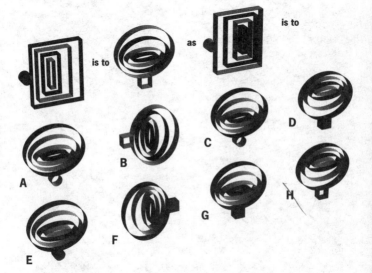

see answer 142

Which of the following is the odd one out?

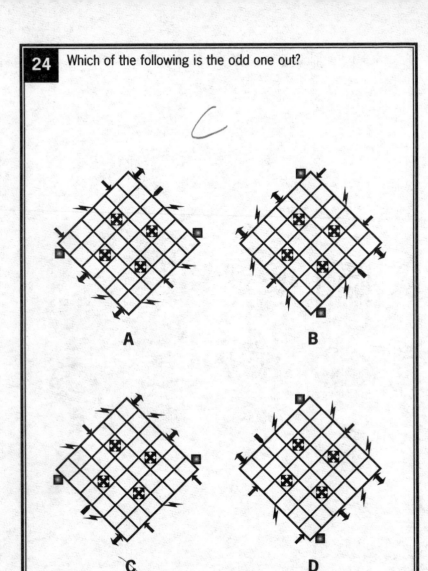

A

B

C

D

see answer 163

There is something wrong with one of the items in a set. Which one?

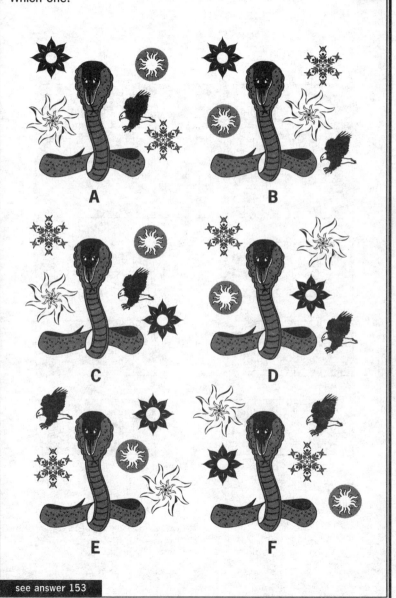

A

B

C

D

E

F

see answer 153

26 Complete the addition.

If [grid] + [grid] = [grid]

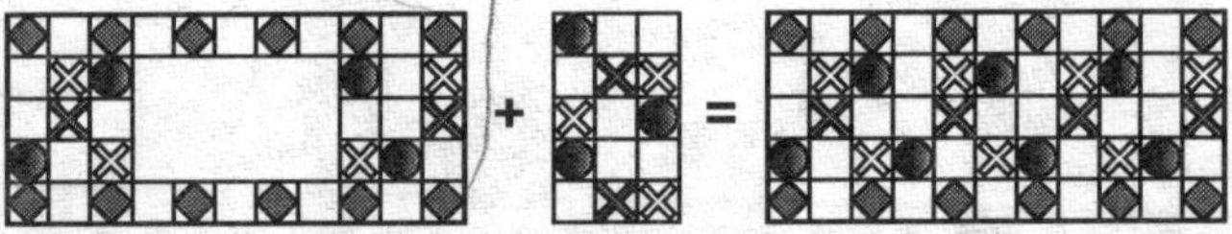

Then [grid] + [grid] = **?**

A [grid]   B [grid]

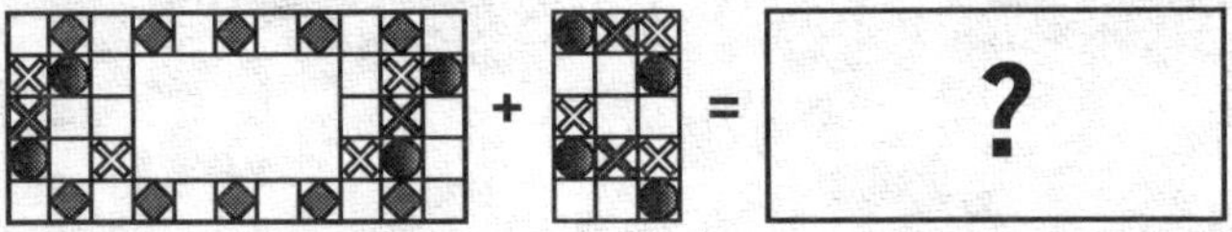

C [grid]   D [grid]

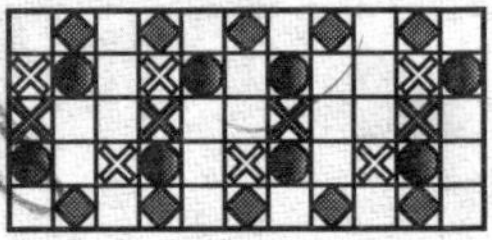

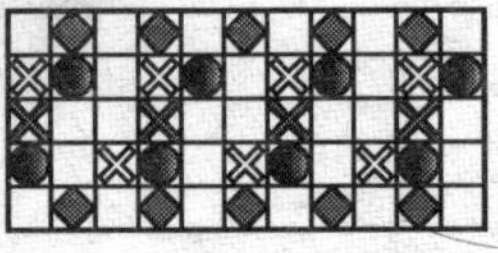

E [grid]   F [grid]

see answer 131

Which tile should replace the question mark? The top and bottom boxes may move independently of each other.

  ?

A   B   C   D

see answer 109

Complete the analogy.

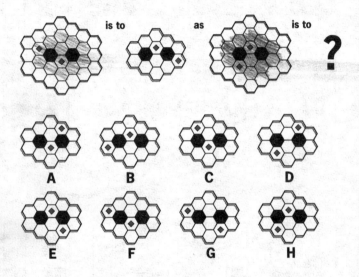

is to   as   is to   **?**

A   B   C   D

E   F   G   H

see answer 87

Find the 8 differences in picture B.

29

A

B

see answer 65

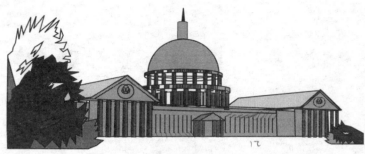

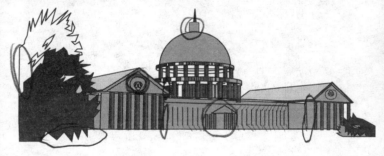

30 Find the two shapes that don't go with the other three.

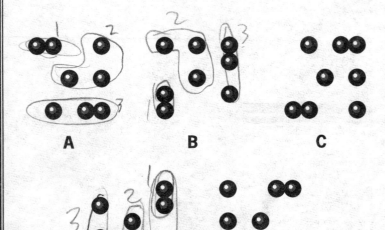

A   B   C

D   E

see answer 44

40

This system is in balance. The black block weighs the same **31**
as the pale blocks. If three more blocks are placed on the
black block, where should two pale blocks be placed to
return the system to balance?

see answer 23

Which of the following is the odd one out?

A   B

C   D

see answer 2

Only two of these butterflies are identical. Which are they?

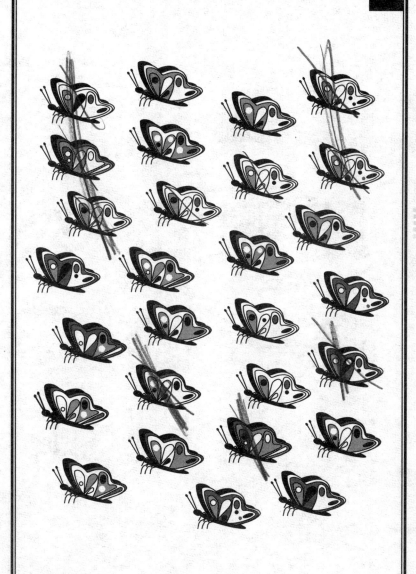

see answer 13

Which is the missing panel?

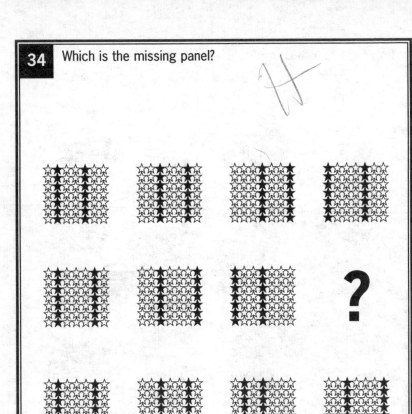

A   B   C   D

E   F   G   H

see answer 138

31

see answer 55

36 Complete the analogy.

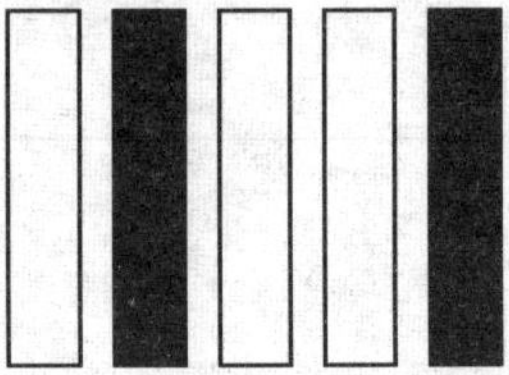

is to

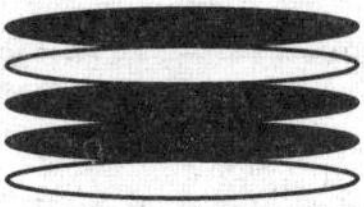

as

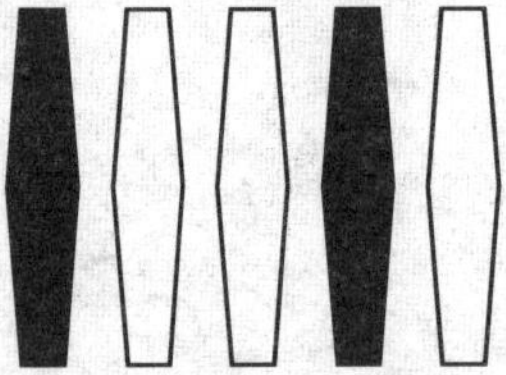

is to

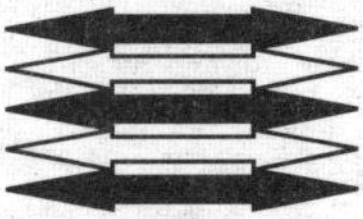

A B  C

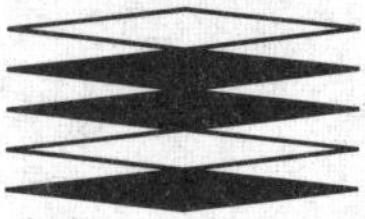

D E  F

see answer 77

Which two patterns do not go with the other three?

37

A

B

they're
all diff.

C

D

E

see answer 99

38 Which tile comes next in this series?

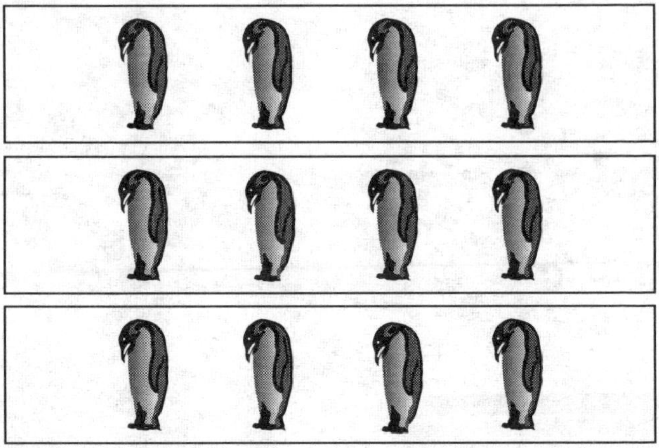

A

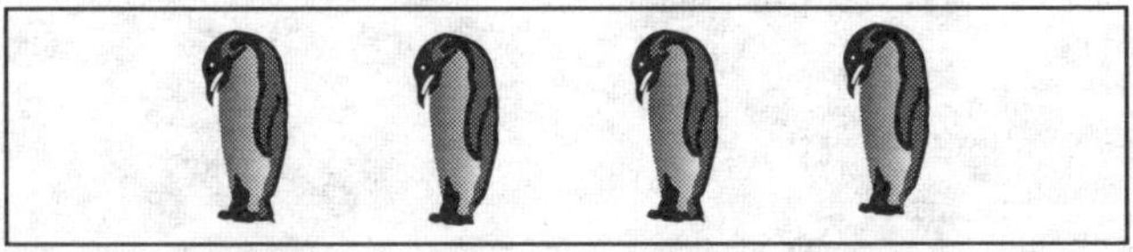

B

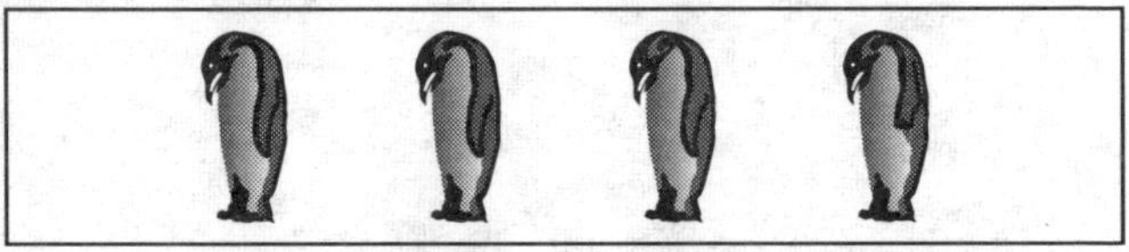

C

D

see answer 121

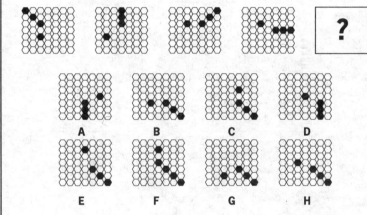

see answer 143

49

40 If the wheel at A is turned as indicated, will the load first rise, or fall?

rise

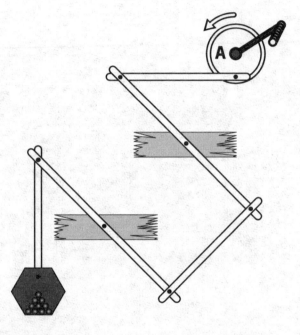

see answer 164

If a brick is dropped from the top of a cliff (on a planet with no atmosphere) at the same time that a projectile is fired parallel with the ground from a large gun, will:

(a) they reach the ground together?

(b) the brick land first?

(c) the projectile land first?

see answer 154

Which of the following is the odd one out?

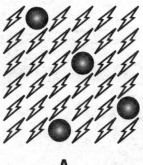

A

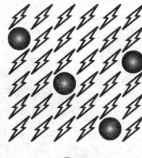

B

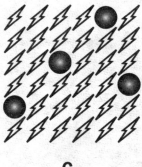

C

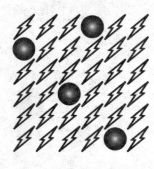

D

see answer 132

The black dots represent hinge points. If points A and B are moved together, will points C and D move together or apart?

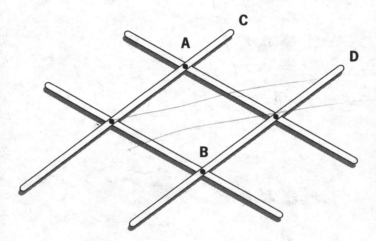

see answer 110

Which of the following is the odd one out?

A

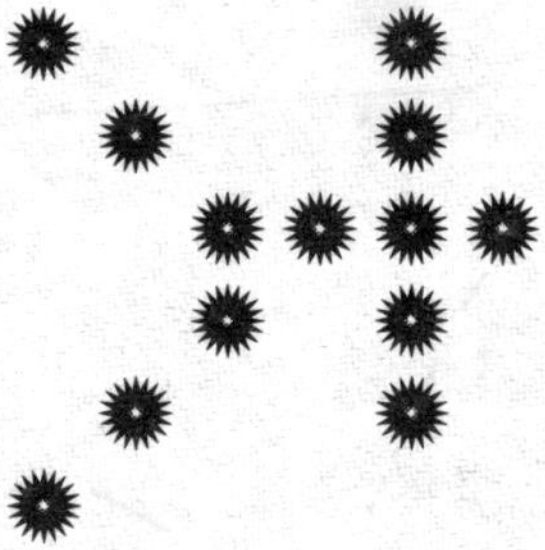

B

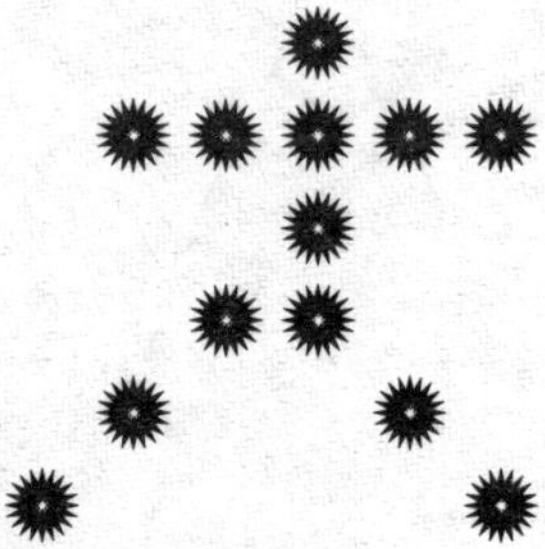

C

D

see answer 88

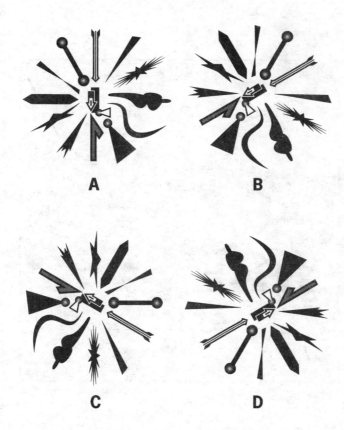

see answer 66

46 Draw four straight lines that divide this puzzle into seven sections, with 3 pyramids and 7 balls in each section. The lines do not have to go from one edge to another.

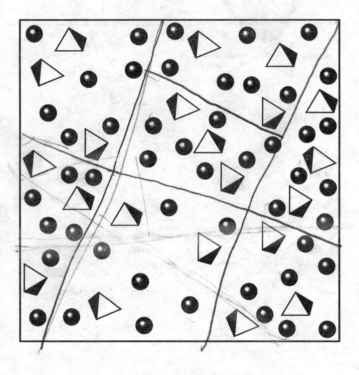

see answer 150

Which set of shapes fits into the middle of this panel to complete the pattern?

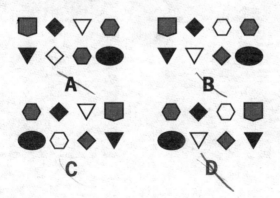

see answer 24

Which of the following make three pairs of identical scenes?

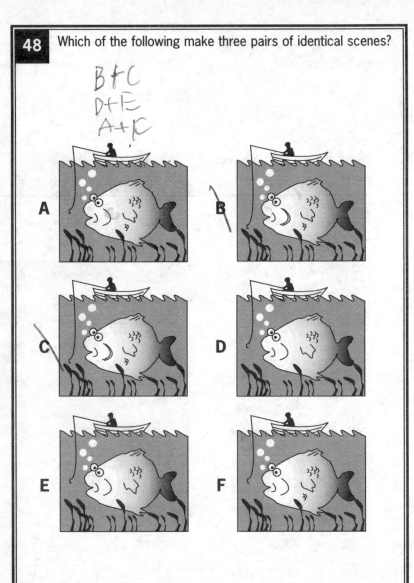

see answer 3

Which of the following is the odd one out?

A

B

C

D

see answer 14

50

Find the 8 places where the routes meet to form cross-roads rather than crossovers.

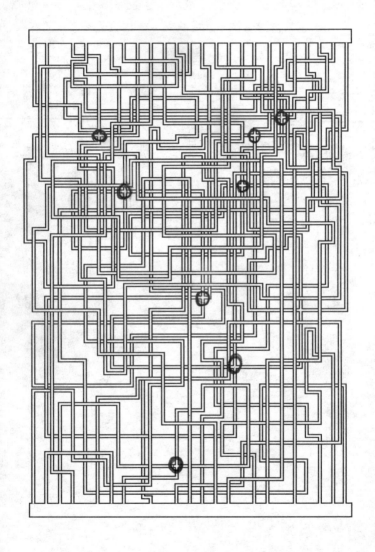

see answer 35

Here is a long multiplication sum worked out. Each symbol represents a number from 0 to 9, and each like symbol always represents the same number. With this in mind, which symbol should replace the question mark?

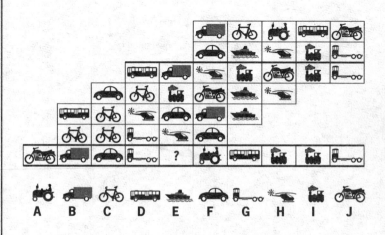

A   B   C   D   E   F   G   H   I   J

see answer 56

61

Which of the following is the odd one out?

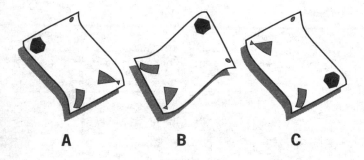

A   **B**   **C**

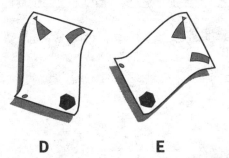

D   **E**

see answer 78

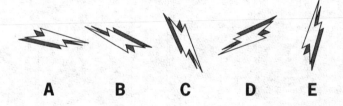

What comes next in this series?

?

A   B   C   D   E

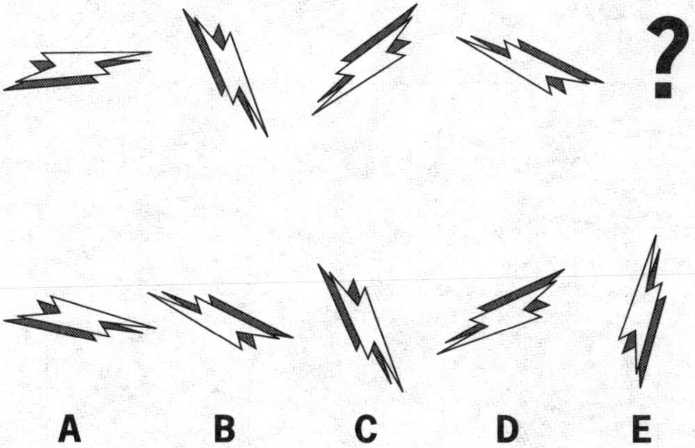

see answer 100

Complete the analogy.

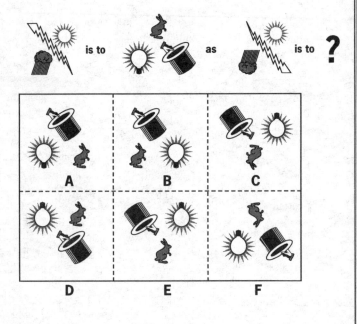

A

B

C

D

E

F

see answer 122

What would this pyramid look like opened out?

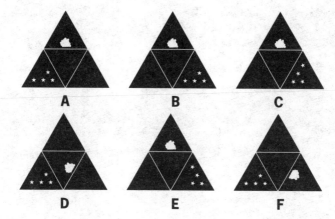

A   B   C

D   E   F

see answer 144

56 Which two of these form an identical pair that do not go with the other eight?

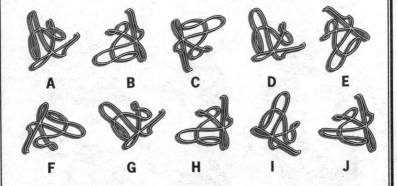

A B C D E

F G H I J

see answer 165

In this system of levers and rods the spots are fixed pivot points and the squares are non-fixed junction points. With this in mind, if the lever is pushed as shown, will the load rise or fall?

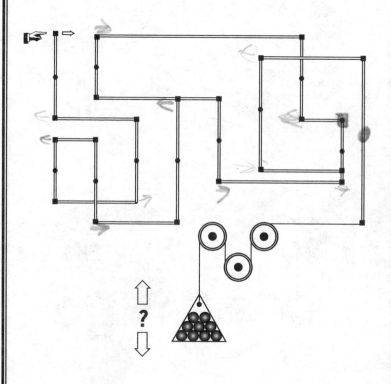

see answer 155

58 Which of the following is the odd one out?

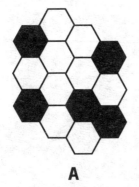

A

B

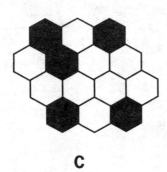

C

D

see answer 133

From the information given, work out the missing total and the values of the different images.

⊙ + ● − ○ = 1

● + ◎ − ⊙ = 5

○ + ◉ − ⊙ = 6

◉ + ○ − ● = 4

| 14 | 15 | ? |

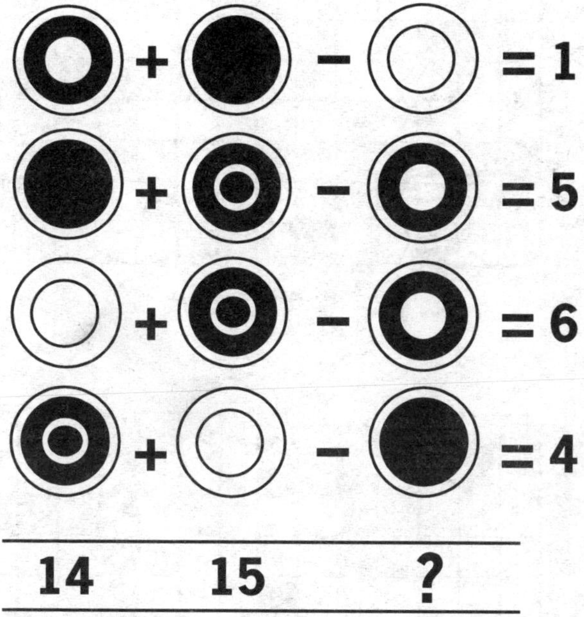

see answer 111

Which of the following is the odd one out?

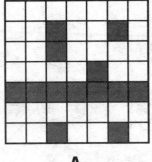

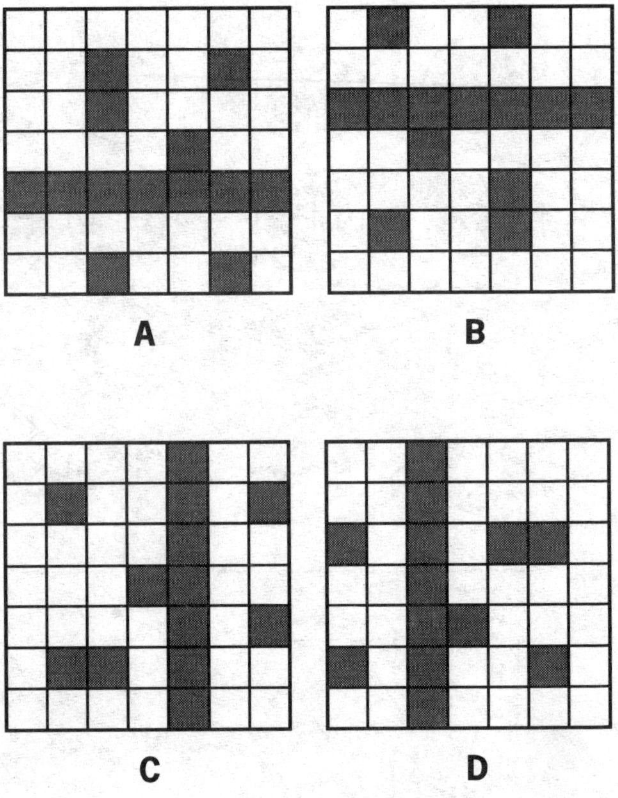

A

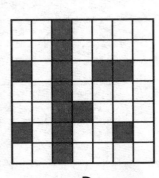

B

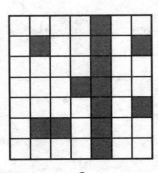

C

D

see answer 89

What comes next in this series?

61

A **B** **C** **D**

see answer 67

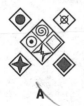

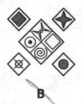

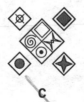

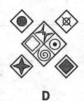

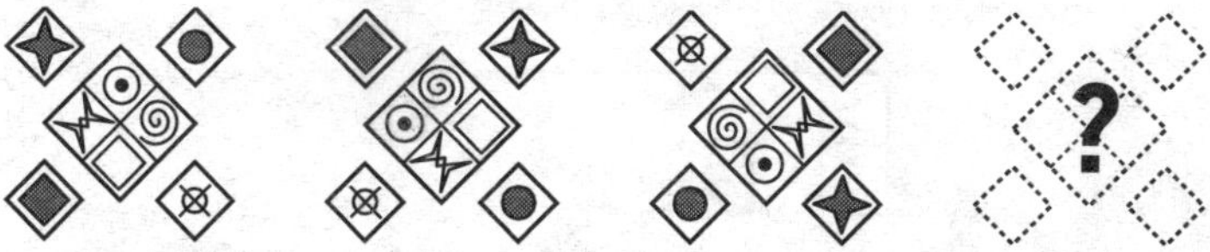

62 Which figure or figures below is or are identical to the one in the box?

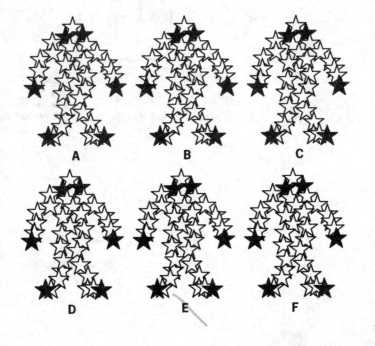

A   B   C

D   E   F

see answer 46

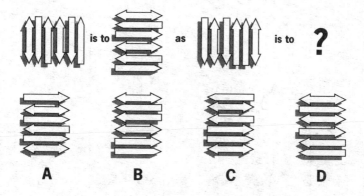

A   B   C   D

see answer 25

Which pattern below can be used to make the box in the middle?

A

B

C

D

see answer 4

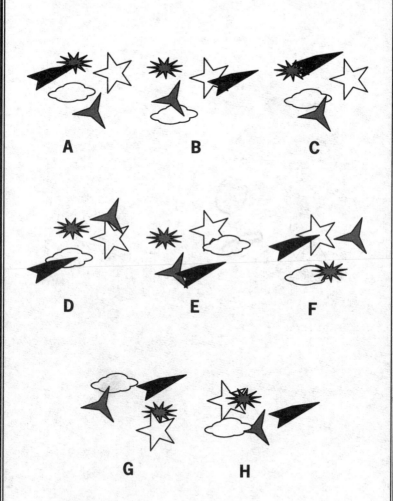

A

B

C

D

E

F

G

H

see answer 15

66 Mark the 9 differences in picture B.

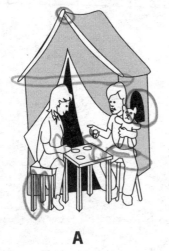

A

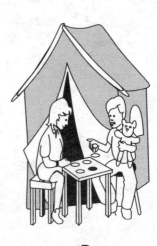

B

see answer 36

What comes next in this series?

67

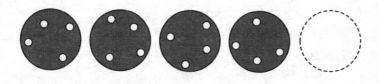

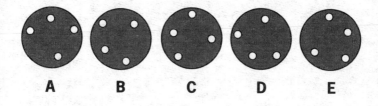

A B C D E

see answer 57

68 Draw three straight lines that divide this puzzle into four sections with, 4, 5, 6 and 7 each of snakes, drums and clouds in respective sections. The lines do not have to go from one edge to another.

see answer 101

Each like animal has the same value and the bear, horse, fish and bird all have different values. Which of A, B, C, D, E or F is the total value of the single column above the question mark, and what are the lowest possible values of the animals?

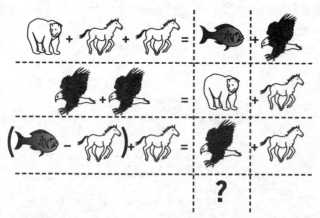

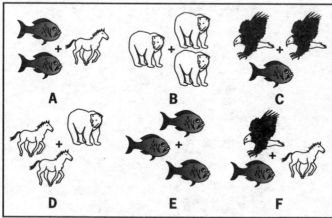

A **B** **C**

D **E** **F**

see answer 123

70 As park ranger on this safari you have to collect as many rattlesnakes as possible without the risk of getting killed or maimed by the other creatures. The bears and wildcats have marked one segment next to the one they stand on, but you have no way of knowing which one, so you may not pass over or next to one. You may not go back over your tracks. Start on the shaded sector and finish on the snake facing to the left.

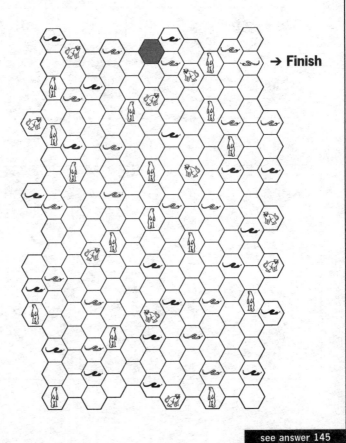

→ **Finish**

see answer 145

Which of the following is the odd one out?

see answer 166

72 Which one of these strings leads you from the perimiter to the diamond?

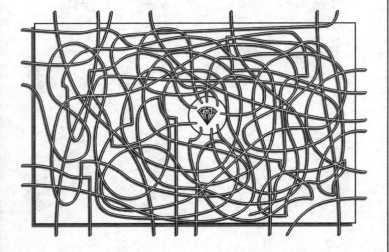

see answer 172

A

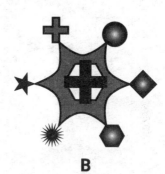

B

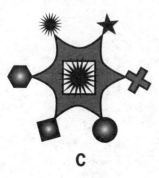

C

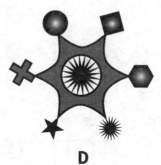

D

see answer 134

Which tile is missing from the following panel?

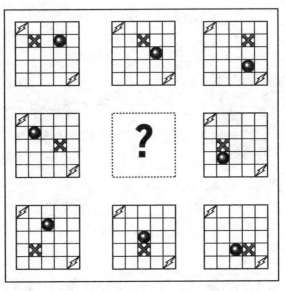

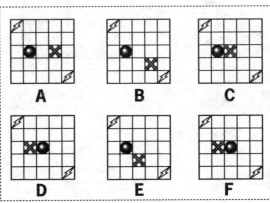

A B C

D E F

see answer 112

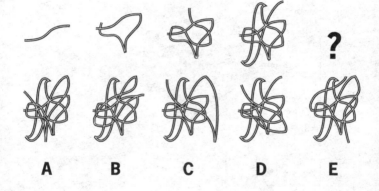

A   B   C   D   E

see answer 90

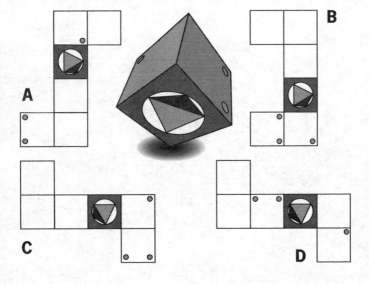

see answer 68

Which set does not go with the other three?

77

see answer 47

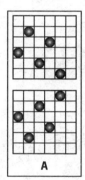

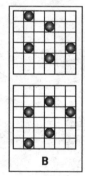

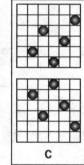

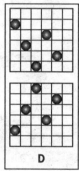

What comes next in this series?

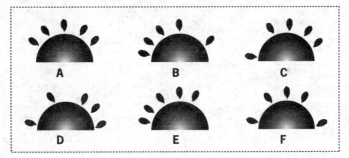

see answer 26

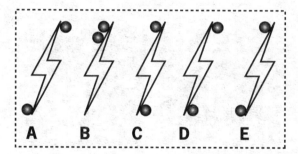

A   B   C   D   E

see answer 5

Which of the following is the odd one out?

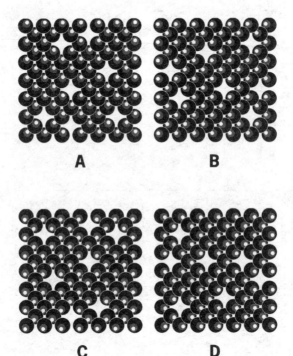

A

B

C

D

see answer 79

Which set should the replace the question mark to complete the pattern?

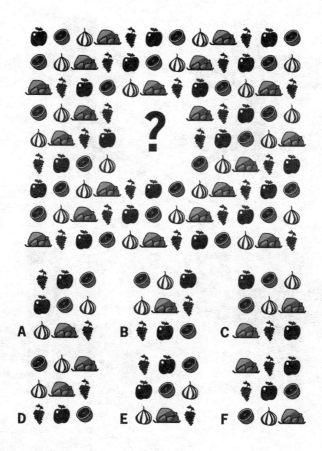

see answer 16

83 Which of the following is the odd one out?

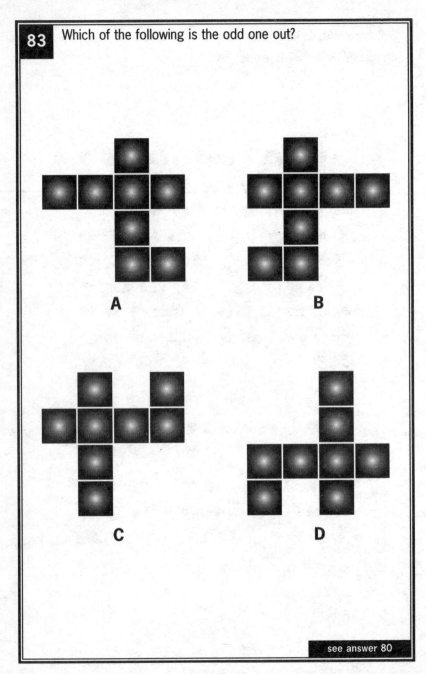

A

B

C

D

see answer 80

Which set of tiles goes into the middle to complete
the pattern?

see answer 58

Which panel should replace the question mark?

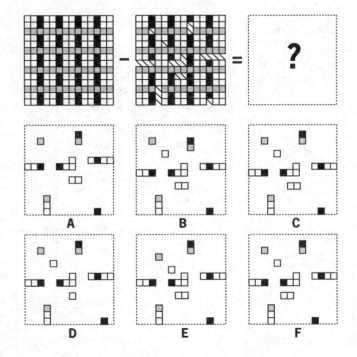

see answer 102

Which of the following is the odd one out?

A

B

C

D

see answer 124

Which tile comes next in this series?

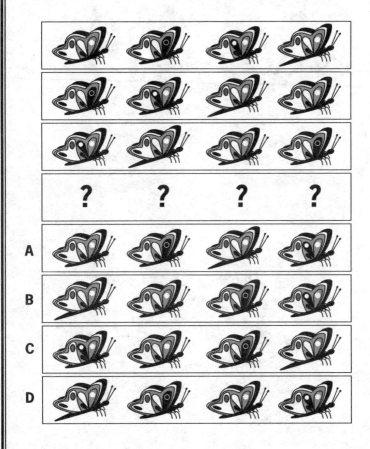

see answer 146

In this system of levers and rollers, in which the crosses are non-fixed junctions and the black spots are fixed pivot points, if the lever is pushed as shown, will each load at A and B rise or fall?

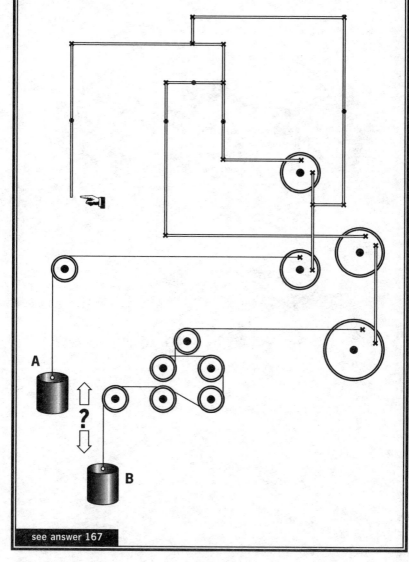

A

B

see answer 167

Which of the following is the odd one out?

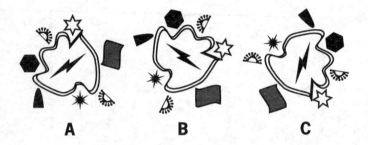

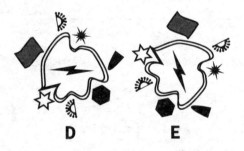

see answer 156

Draw three straight lines that divide this puzzle into six sections that contain 1 fish and 1 flag in each and respectively 0, 1, 2, 3, 4 and 5 drums and lightning bolts. The lines do not have to go from one edge to another.

see answer 135

91 The symbols in the following calculations represent the numbers from 0 to 9. Each like symbol always represents the same number. What symbol should replace the question mark?

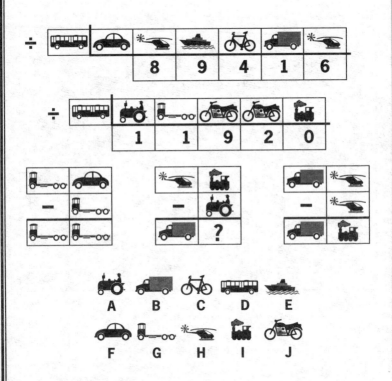

see answer 113

What should replace the question mark?

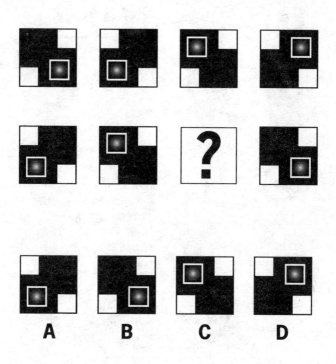

see answer 45

101

93 In this system of fixed belts and freely revolving pulley wheels, what will happen to the loads A and B when the handle is turned in the direction indicated?

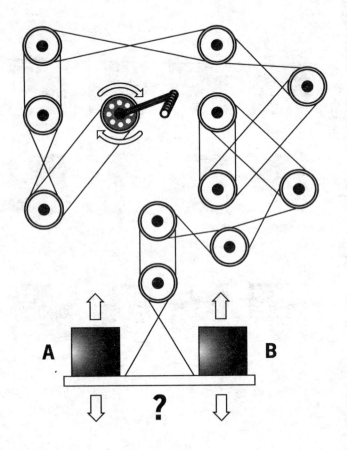

A

B

?

see answer 69

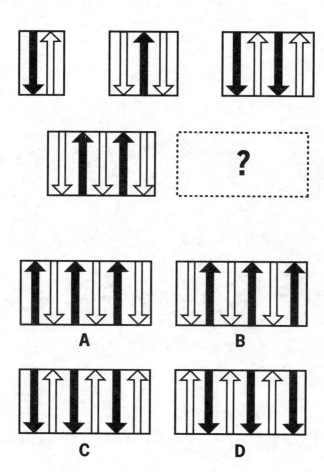

see answer 48

What comes next in this series?

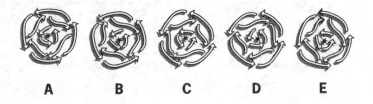

A   B   C   D   E

see answer 27

Complete the analogy.

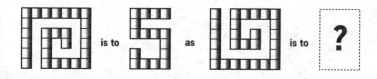

is to   as   is to   ?

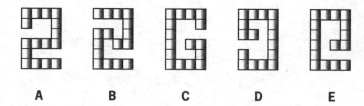

A   B   C   D   E

see answer 6

Which of the following is the odd one out?

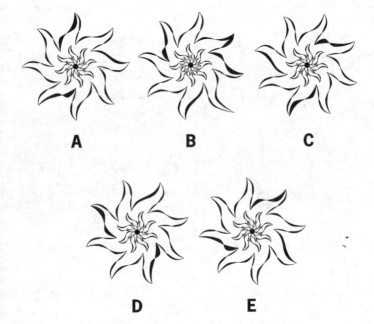

A   B   C

D   E

see answer 17

Find the 14 differences in picture B.

98

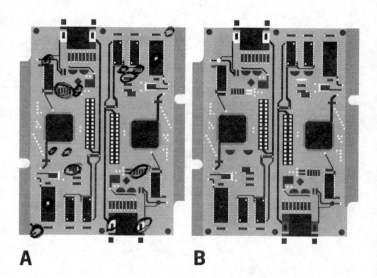

A　　　　　**B**

see answer 38

What should replace the question mark?

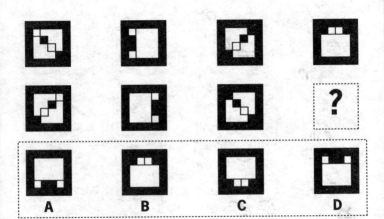

see answer 59

Find the only continuous route from the left of this puzzle to the right.

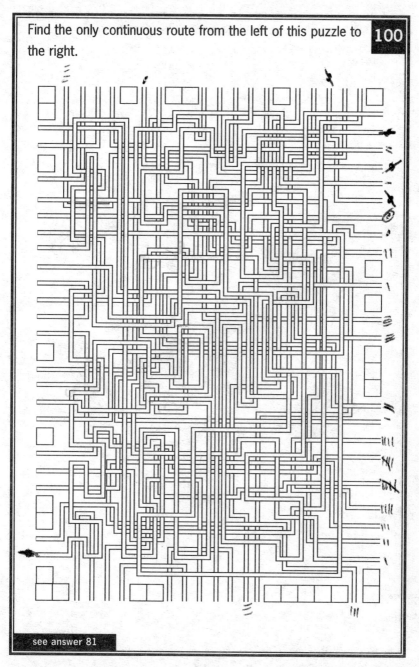

see answer 81

101 Which of the surrounding pieces fits perfectly on top of the middle piece to make a rectangular block?

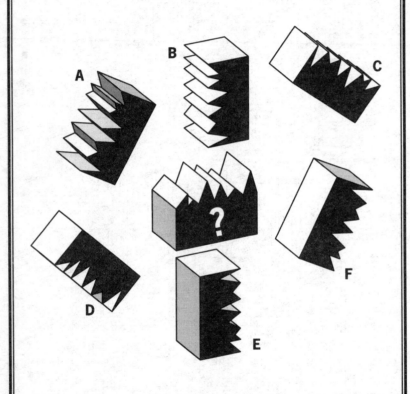

see answer 103

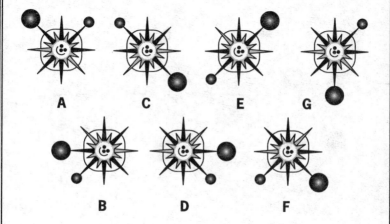

see answer 125

Which objects should replace the question marks?

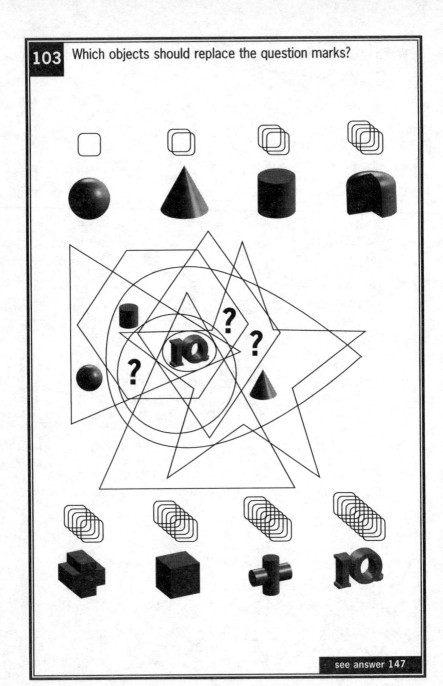

see answer 147

Which of the surrounding shapes is the box in the middle opened out?

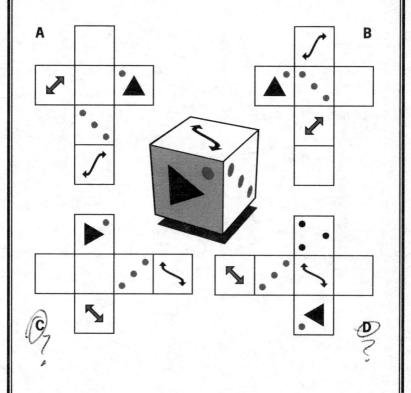

A

B

C

D

see answer 168

Complete the analogy.

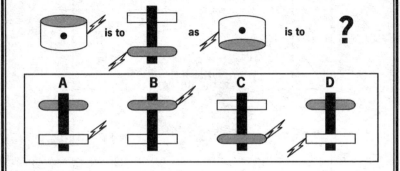

see answer 157

Which of the following is the odd one out?

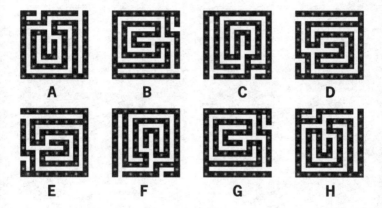

see answer 136

115

107 In this system of pulley wheels and levers, where the black spots are fixed pivots and the crosses are non-fixed junctions, will (A) rise or fall and will (B) rise or fall when the wheel at the top is turned in the direction indicated.

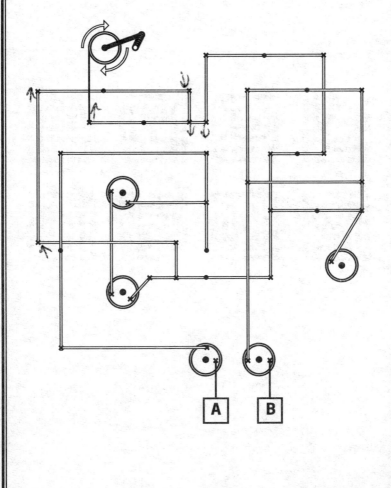

see answer 114

Which of the figures below is the same as the one in the box?

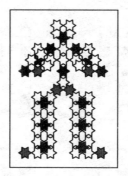

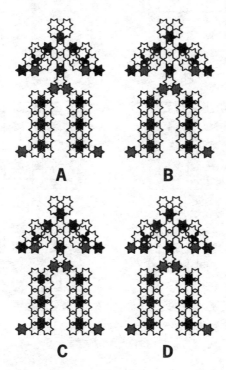

A

B

C

D

see answer 92

Which of the following is the odd one out?

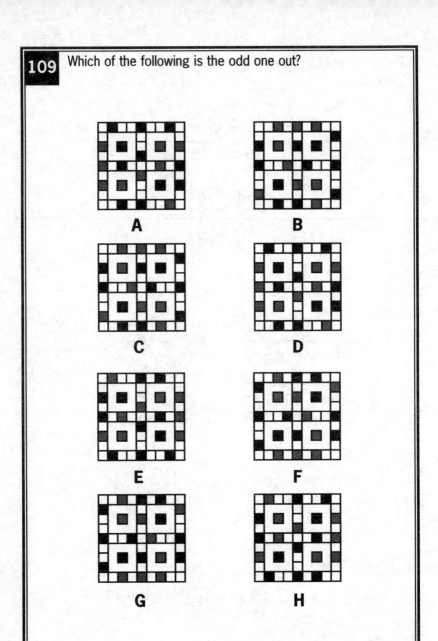

A

B

C

D

E

F

G

H

see answer 70

Draw five straight lines that divide this puzzle into six sections that have 1 chimp, 1 koala, 3 snakes, 4 dogs and 5 stars in each section. The lines do not have to go from one edge to another.

see answer 49

Which of the following is the odd one out?

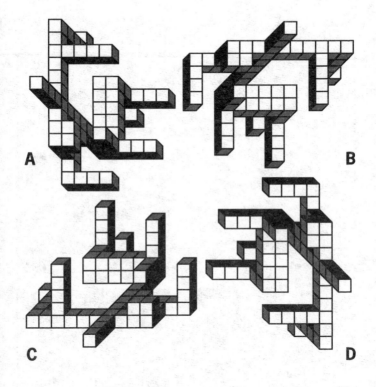

A

B

C

D

see answer 28

Which of the figures below should replace the question mark in the box?

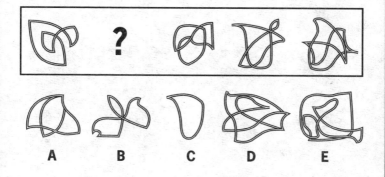

A   B   C   D   E

see answer 7

Complete the analogy?

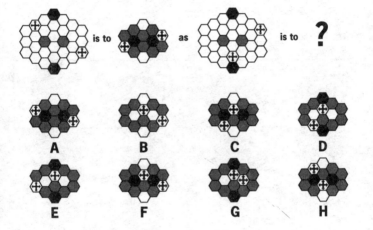

see answer 18

A black block below weighs three times a white block. Where should one black box be placed to return this system to balance?

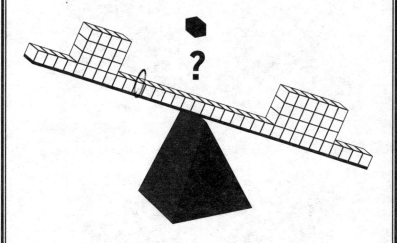

see answer 39

Which of the following is the odd one out?

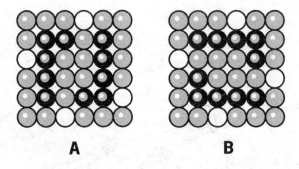

A   B

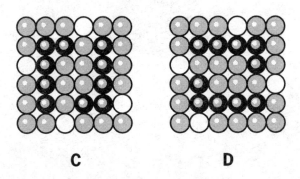

C   D

see answer 60

Find the 10 horse & carriage sets hidden behind these vehicles.

see answer 82

Which of the following is the odd one out?

A

B

C

D

see answer 104

What comes next in this series?

118

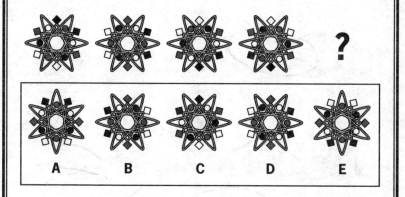

see answer 126

What would this pyramid look like opened out?

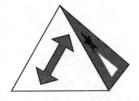

A

B

C

D

E

F

see answer 148

In this system of cogs, levers and pulley wheels, in which the black spots are fixed pivot points and the crosses are non-fixed junctions, the loads at A and B are in balance. Which one will rise when the wheel at the bottom is turned as indicated?

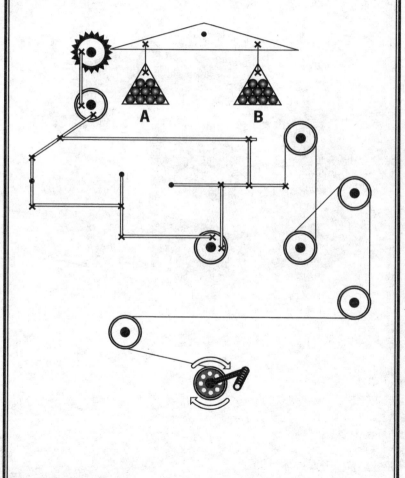

A   B

see answer 169

121 Which of the surrounding pieces fits perfectly on top of the middle piece to make a rectangular block.

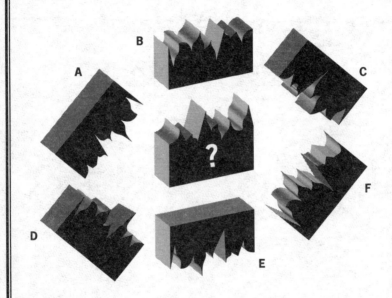

see answer 158

What comes next in this series? **122**

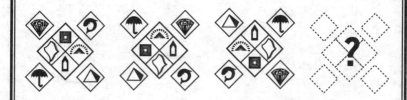

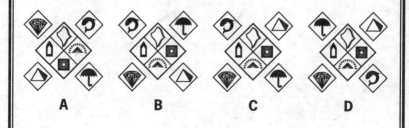

A B C D

see answer 137

Which tile is missing from this series of panels?

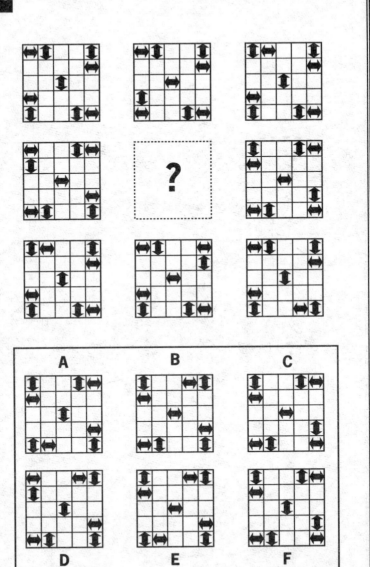

A   B   C

D   E   F

see answer 115

Which of the following is the odd one out?

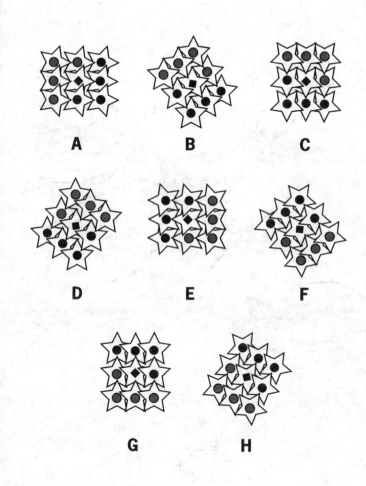

A

B

C

D

E

F

G

H

see answer 93

Which two of these images are identical?

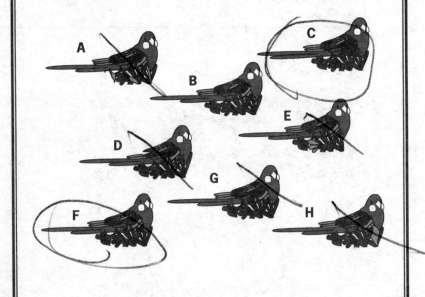

A

B

C

D

E

F

G

H

see answer 71

Find the 12 differences in picture B.

B

A

see answer 50

What is the missing set?

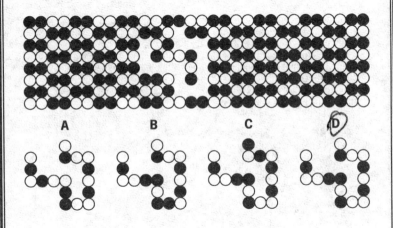

A   B   C   D

see answer 29

Map out the route to the diamond using the key below. Follow the direction of the apex of the triangle; for example the triangle to the right of Start is pointing right, so you should go 6 squares right. You may travel forward, back, up or down, but not diagonally nor retrace your steps, although your path may criss-cross.

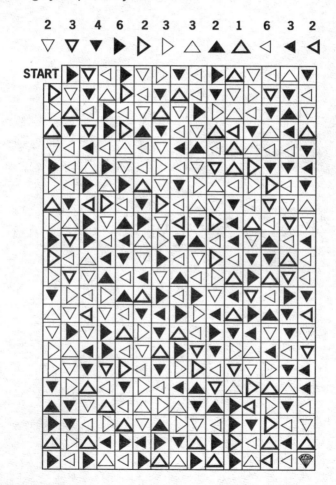

see answer 8

137

Draw three lines that connect the next three drums in sequence with the boxes they should go in.

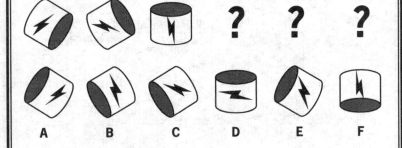

A B C D E F

see answer 19

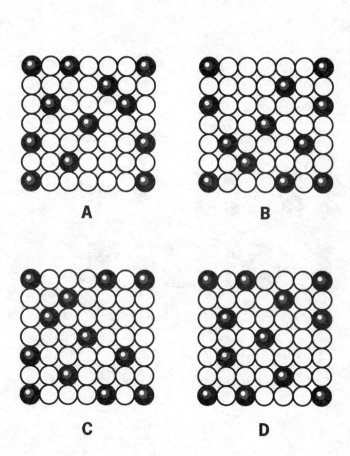

A

B

C

D

see answer 40

Complete the analogy.

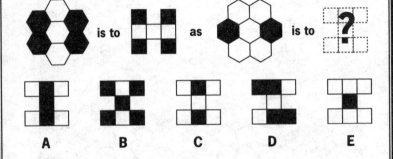

A   B   C   D   E

see answer 61

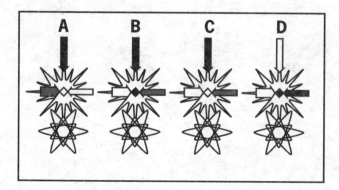

see answer 83

What is the missing set?

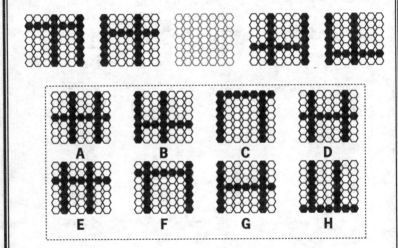

see answer 105

142

38

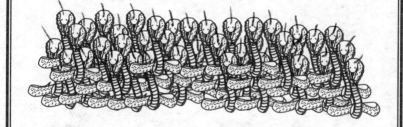

see answer 127

135 Draw three straight lines that make four sections with a total value of 40 in each, using the values given below. The lines do not have to go from one edge to another.

0   1   2   3   4   5

see answer 149

Which of the following is the odd one out?

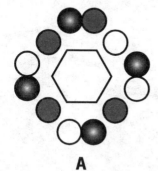

A

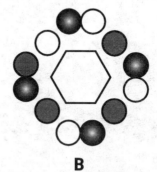

B

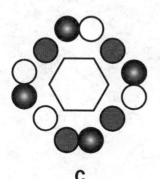

C

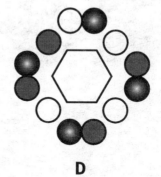

D

see answer 170

Which of the following is the odd one out?

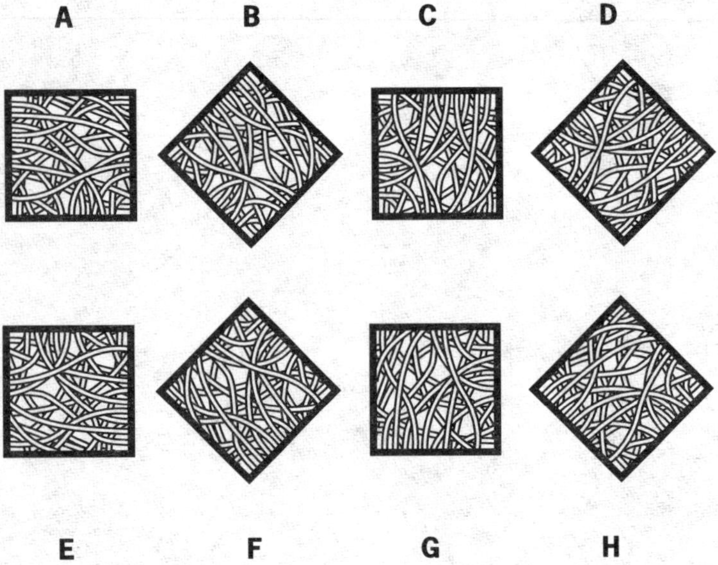

A   B   C   D

E   F   G   H

see answer 159

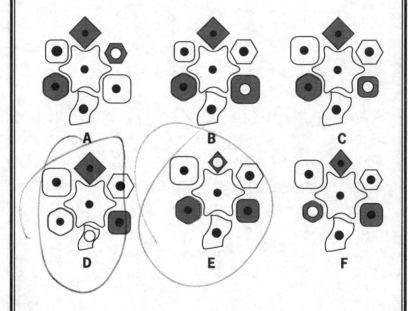

see answer 34

In this system of cogs, levers and rollers, in which the black spots are fixed pivot points and the crosses are non-fixed junctions, does the load at A and the load at B rise or drop when the lever at the top is pushed as shown?

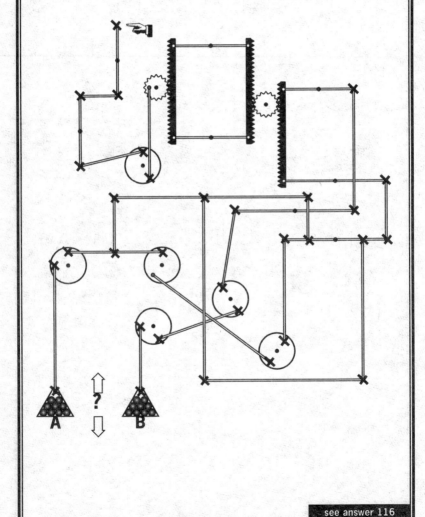

see answer 116

Each animal keeps the same value and the leopard, flea, dog and rabbit all have different values. Which of A, B, C, D, E or F is the total value of the single column above the question mark, and what are the lowest possible values of the animals?

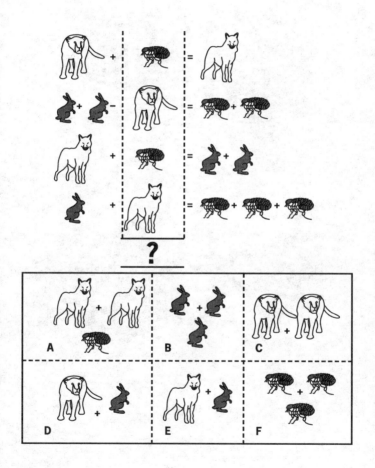

see answer 94

Which of the following is the odd one out?

A

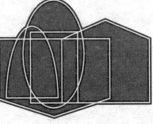

B

C

D

see answer 72

What are the 8 differences in picture B?

142

A

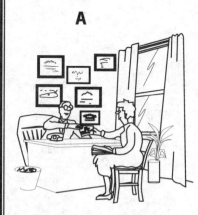

B

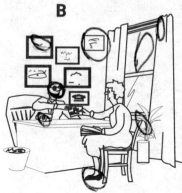

see answer 51

Complete the analogy.

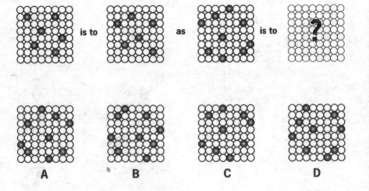

A   B   C   D

see answer 30

What comes next in this series?

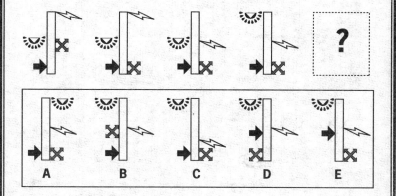

see answer 9

153

Find the only route from the perimeter of this field to the diamond at the center.

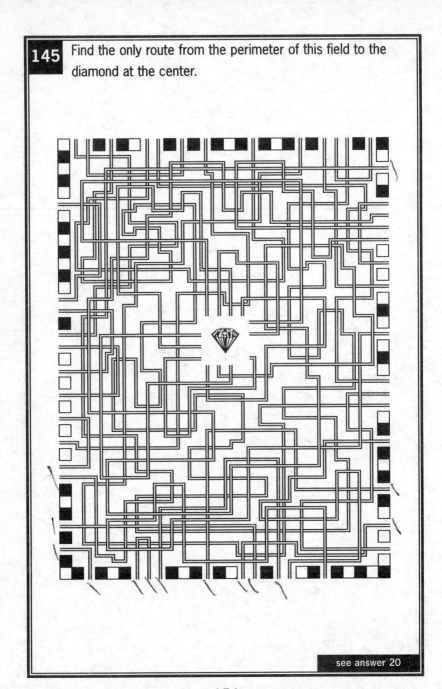

see answer 20

Find the odd one out in each row.

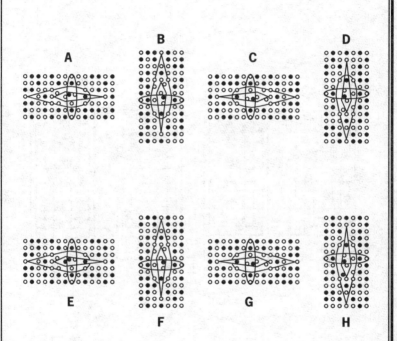

A

B

C

D

E

F

G

H

see answer 41

Which of the following is the odd one out?

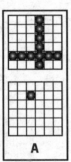 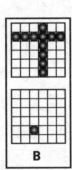 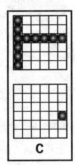 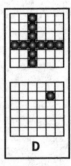

A B C D

see answer 62

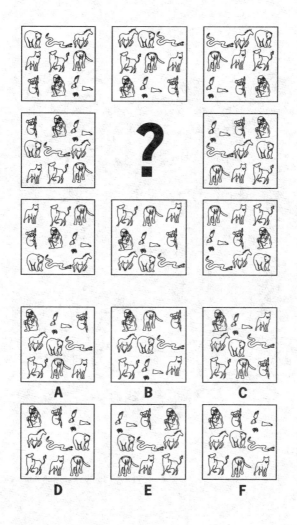

see answer 84

Which of the following is the odd one out?

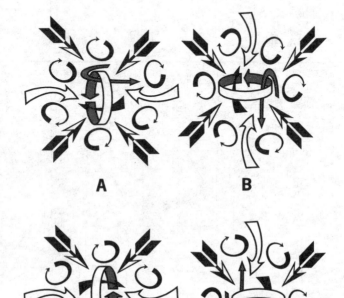

A

B

C

D

see answer 173

When the cube in the middle is opened out, which of the surrounding shapes does it make?

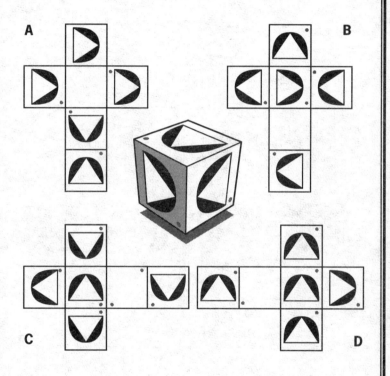

A

B

C

D

see answer 106

Complete the analogy.

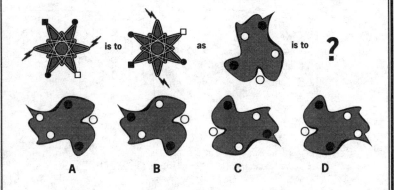

is to ... as ... is to **?**

A   B   C   D

see answer 128

Which of the surrounding shapes fits exactly onto the middle piece to make a rectangular block?

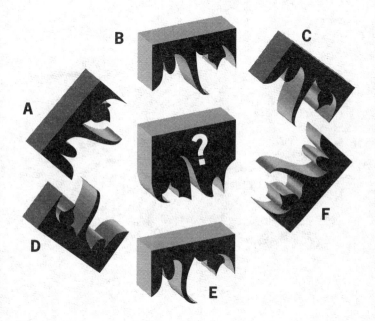

see answer 91

Which clock is the odd-one-out?

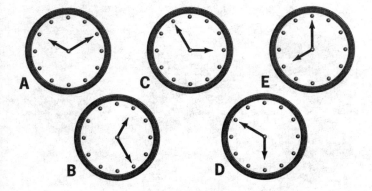

A   C   E

B   D

see answer 171

Which of the following is the odd one out?

A   **B**

C   **D**

see answer 174

Which jet fighter is missing?

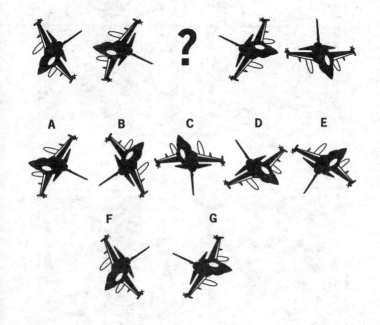

A   B   C   D   E

F   G

see answer 160

Which of the following is the odd one out?

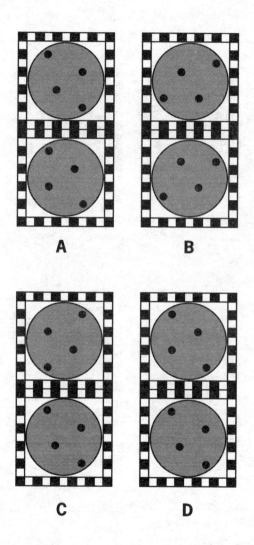

A

B

C

D

see answer 139

Which panel should replace the question mark?

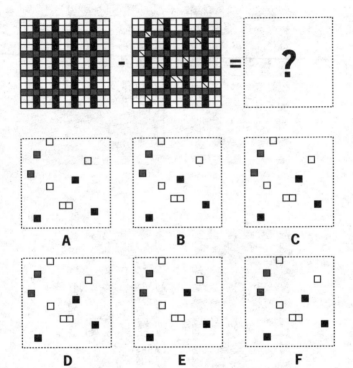

see answer 117

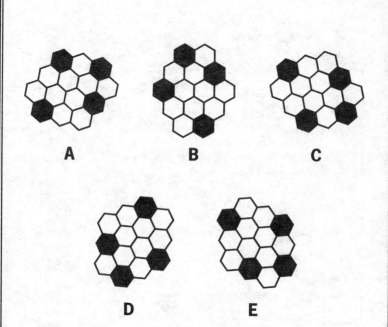

A

B

C

D

E

see answer 95

159 Draw four straight lines that divide this puzzle into five sections with 1 scuba diver, 3 fish and respectively, 4, 5, 6, 7 and 8 large bubbles and sea shells in each section. The lines do not have to go from one edge to another.

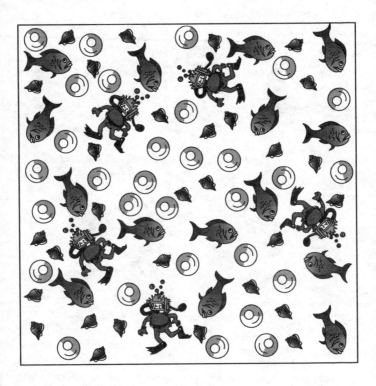

see answer 73

Which of the following is the odd one out?

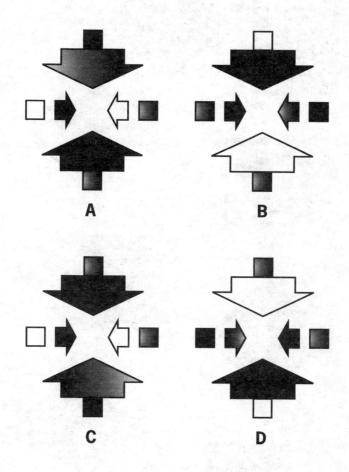

A

B

C

D

see answer 52

Which two are the odd ones out?

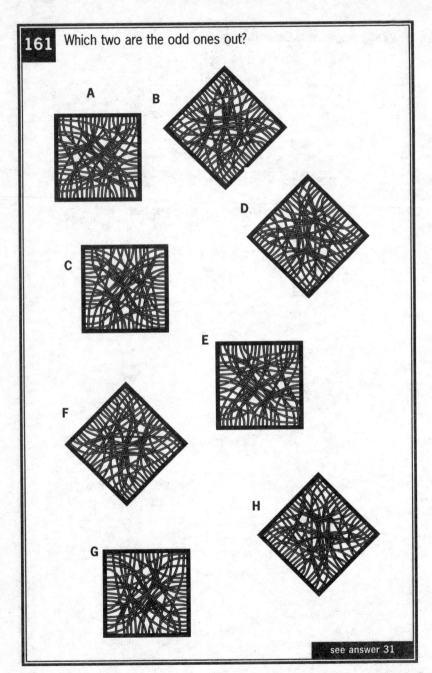

A

B

C

D

E

F

G

H

see answer 31

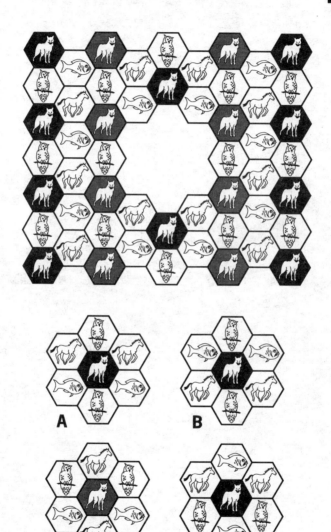

163 These ramps are fixed in position. When the ball at the top is released, where will it eventually come to rest?

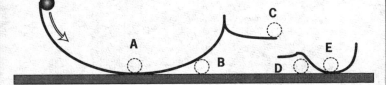

see answer 21

This system is in balance. The load at B is on a plank which **164** sits on top of two rollers. The black spots are fixed pivot points and the crosses are non-fixed junctions. When the lever at the bottom is pushed as shown, will the load at A rise or fall and will the load at B move left or right?

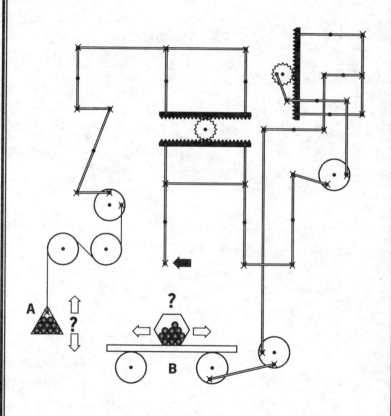

A

?

B

see answer 42

173

Complete the analogy.

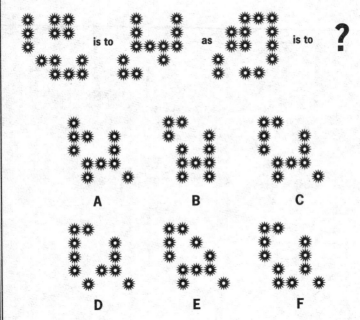

A

B

C

D

E

F

see answer 63

What comes next in this series?

166

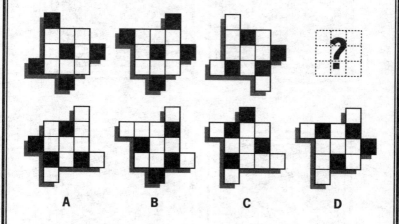

A B C D

see answer 85

Which of the following is the odd one out?

A

B

C

D

see answer 107

Each like symbol has the same value throughout. What is the missing symbol? Clue: the small numbers are numbers carried when adding.

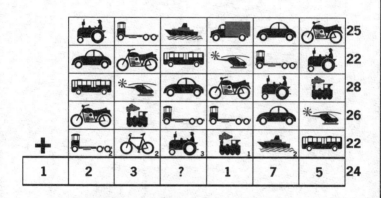

A B C D E

F G H I J

see answer 129

169 Find the 13 differences in picture B.

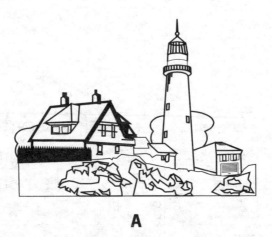

A

B

see answer 151

170

Which of the following is the odd one out?

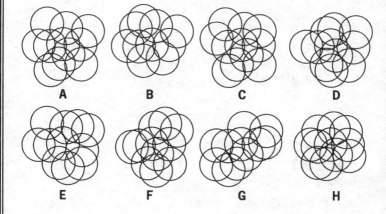

A B C D

E F G H

see answer 161

What should replace the question mark?

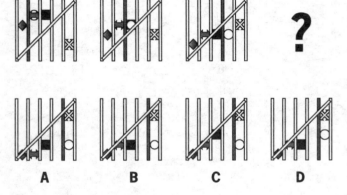

?

A   **B**   **C**   **D**

see answer 140

Complete the analogy.

 is to

as 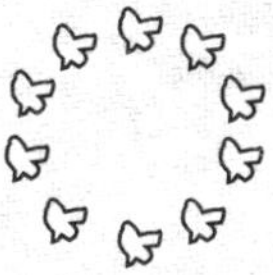 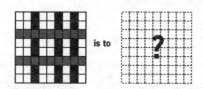 is to

A    B   C   D

see answer 118

173 Which path will the bomb take when released from this moving fighter-bomber on a calm day?

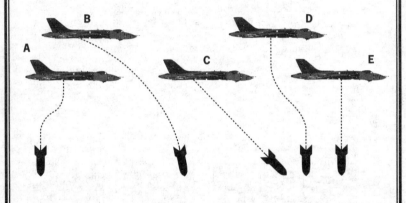

see answer 96

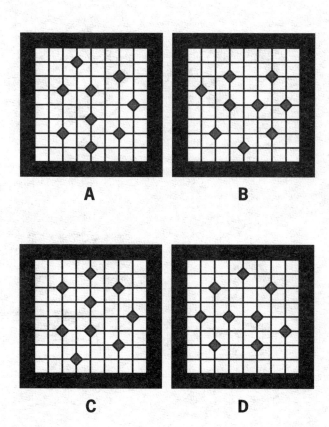

A

B

C

D

see answer 74

Which of the following is the odd one out?

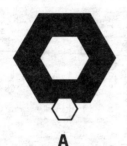

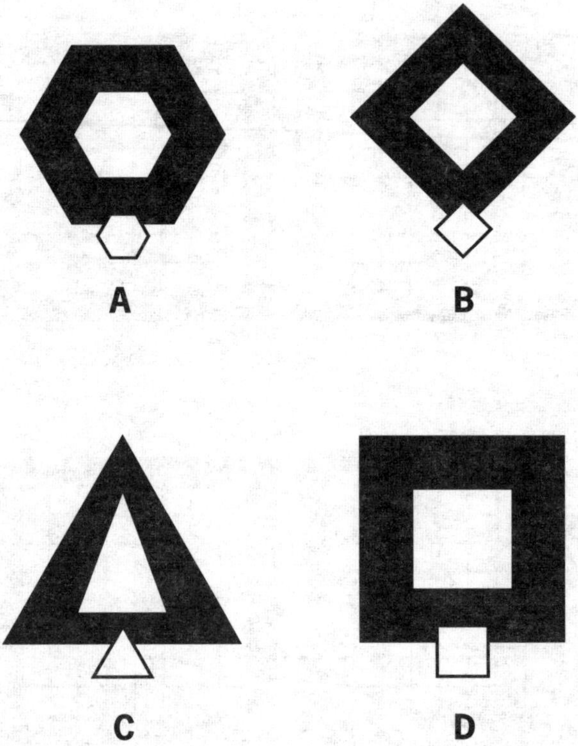

A

B

C

D

see answer 175

1

2   B. The black diamonds have changed position.

3   A & F, B & C, D & E.

4   D.

5   A. From what has gone before we can deduce that one ball goes over to the other side before the next ball moves.

6   A. The analogous pattern is simply upside down.

7   A. The sequence is built according to the number of enclosed spaces in each shape.

8

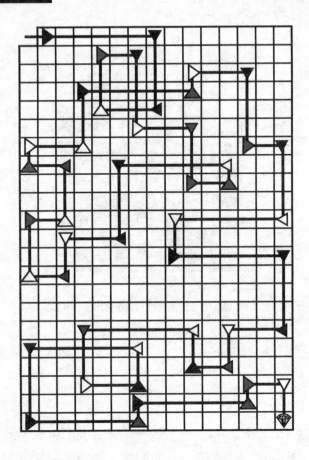

9   E. The objects are rotating around the pole in a clockwise direction; the arrow must move next to make room for the cross to come round.

10   A.

11

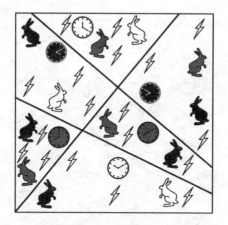

12   Here is proof that it can be done.

13   *See next page.*

14   A. The position of the balls is mirror reversed while the others are rotations of the same positions.

15   A. In all the others there are two pairs of two objects that touch each other.

Answers

[13]   The third on the second column and the fifth on the third
column.

16   C. The series of five foods always retains the same order:
apple, grapefruit, garlic, chicken,grapes.

17   B. There are 3 changes.

18 F. The larger shape is condensed, the whole figure is horizontally flipped and the shading cycles, respectively, from black to white, white to shaded, and shaded to black, except where a cross is present.

19 The lightning bolt and the drum rotate an equal amount clockwise and anti- (counter) clockwise.

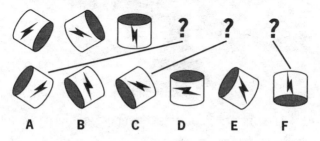

20 Follow the black route.

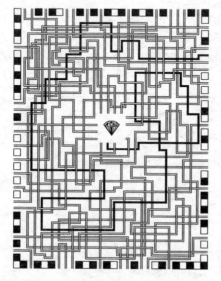

21 A. At the end of the first ramp the ball will be moving vertically, and so will fall back down, eventually coming to rest at the lowest point.

22 B. It is a mirror image inversion of the way the others rotate.

23

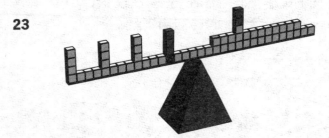

24 C. The same seven objects are repeated continuously in each line, regardless of tone.

25 C. The figure flips onto its right side.

26 B. The pattern rotates two sunrays one step at a time.

27 C. The pattern rotates anti- (counter) clockwise, one tenth of a turn (36°) each step.

28 B. There is a block missing.

29 D.

30 B. The set is turned onto its right side and reflected in the horizontal plane.

31 D and G. The line in black is missing from both.

32 212 blocks (each set has 53).

33 A. The cog and star at the bottom have changed place.

34 B and F. In all others, the white circle is inside the smallest outer shape.

35 The 8 crossroads are marked

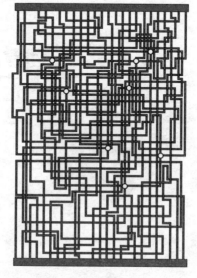

36

37   B. All the others have the same inner and outer shape.

38   *See next page.*

39

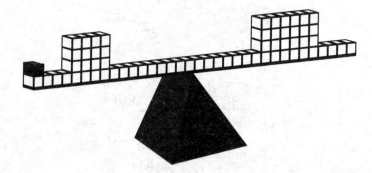

40   D. A black spot has changed position in the third row up.

[38]

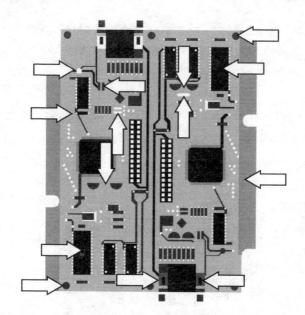

41 C and H. Both have one more white spot and one less black spot.

42 A will fall, B will move to the left.

43 A & B, C & D.

44 C and E. They are mirror images. The others are the same shape in different rotations.

45 D. Starting from the left in each row, the object rolls onto its right side with each move.

46 F. All the others have one or more difference.

47   D. The others are all rotated versions of the same figure on the top half, with the mirror-images on the bottom half, but the mirror-image of D is on top.

48   C. When the black arrows point down, the sequence begins with a black arrow.

49

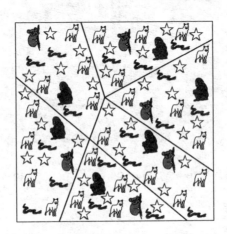

50

Answers

51

52 C. It is the only one which is not a rotation of the shading of the others.

53 A & F.

54 C. It is a mirror image of the way the others rotate.

55 31 kangaroos.

56 *see next page.*

57 B. The spots rotate clockwise one-fifth of a turn (72°) each time.

58 C. The pattern is made from continuously repeating the top row of tiles, rolling back two tiles with each row.

[56] The missing symbol is G, the unladen truck (worth 0).

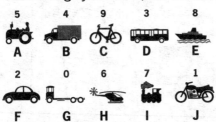

The values and working are as follows:

```
            4  9  5  3  1
         ×  2  8  6  7  0
         ─────────────────
         3  4  6  7  1  7  0
      2  9  7  1  8  6
   3  9  6  2  4  8
   9  9  0  6  2
─────────────────────────
1  4  2  0  0  5  3  7  7  0
```

59 B. Each object in the bottom row is a right-hand mirror-image of the shape above so, in this case, the image will be the same as the object.

60 D. The bottom white spot has changed place with the shaded spot now on its left.

61 C.

62 D. In the other sets the single black spot is in the reflection of the point of intersection of the two black lines. Alternatively, in all the other cases if the single spot is superimposed on the other shape it would join a vertical or horizontal line of black spots.

63 C. Each two halves of the analogy, when put together, make a complete 5 x 5 square.

64 B. Billy's plot has the greatest perimeter.

65 There are eight differences.

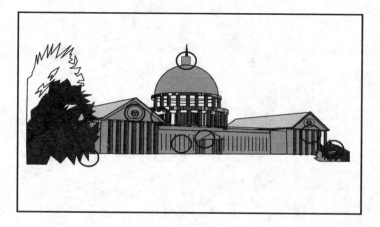

66 D. The triangular shapes have switched position.

67 D. The inner shapes rotate anti-clockwise; the outer shapes rotate clockwise.

68 D.

69 A will rise, B will fall.

70 H. The inner squares have swapped shading. The right-hand column is the left-hand column rotated.

71   B and F.

72   D. Not all the shapes intersect.

73

74   A. This is a mirror-image of the rotation of the other shapes.

75   B. This is a mirror-image of the other shapes.

76   *see next page.*

77   D. The shape is turned on its right side and the shading is reversed.

78   C. The round spot and the rectangle have changed places.

[76] 157 bricks.

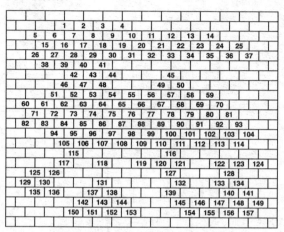

79 D. One of the balls has been displaced relative to the other sets, which are all rotated versions of the same set.

80 B. This is a mirror image of the other shapes, which are all rotated versions of the same object.

81 *see next page.*

82 *see next page.*

83 B. The sequence of arrows rotates anti-clockwise, and the diamond shape in the middle is the same shading as the arrow at the top.

84 A, If the rows were numbered down, the sequence would be 123, 312, 231.

[81] Follow the black route.

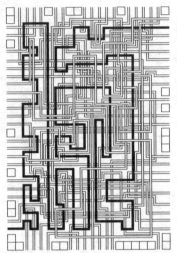

82

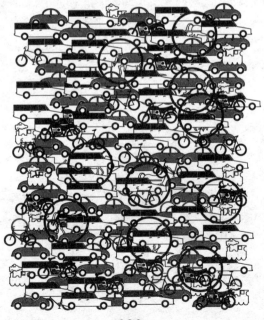

85   B. The second figure is a rotated mirror-image of the first, and so the missing figure is a similarly rotated mirror-image of the third figure.

86   B and C.

87   A. The diamonds rotate around the centre point.

88   B. This is a mirror-image of the rotation of the others.

89   C. Various blocks have been displaced in relation to the other shapes.

90   B. The sequence always adds two double-curved lines onto the end of the previous pattern, at the end of the last new point added.

91   C.

92   B.

93   D. The shape rotates one-eighth of a turn (45°) each time, but in D the topmost black dot is swapped with the grey dot opposite.

94   A. The values are:

leopard = 3;   flea = 2;
dog = 5;   rabbit = 4.

The sums are:

2 + 3 [5] = 5;
(4 + 4) − 2 [6] = 3 + 3 [6];
4 + 5 [9] = 3 + 3 + 3 [9];
the column sum is 3 + 2 + 3 + 5 [13] = dog + dog + flea (5 + 5 + 3 [13]).

95   C. This is a rotated mirror-image of the others.

96   B. The bomb will follow a smooth parabolic curve.

97   A. The pattern rolls vertically and horizontally, in steps of 4.

98   D.The others all go anti-clockwise.

99   D and E. These are rotated mirror images of the other three.

100   E. The shapes rotate 72° clockwise each time.

101

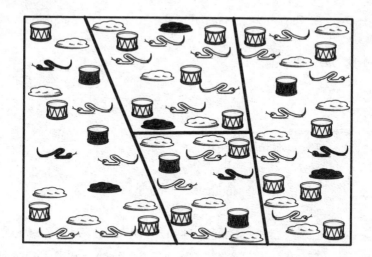

102 C.

103 C.

104 C. The tree has an extra inner shape.

105 D. The black vertical stripes move one column to the right one stripe each time, rolling over as it reaches the end of the shape. The black horizontal stripe moves down one row each time.

106 B.

107 D. The arrow has come to the front of the objects below it.

108 It will drop.

109 D.

110 They will move apart.

111 13. Dove = 2; football = 3; earth = 5; spiral = 4.

112 C. Any cross in the middle column is always in the middle of its left and right positions, and the black spot is always one place below its position in the tile to the left of it.

113 The helicopter (worth 2).

8	1	9	7	5
A	B	C	D	E

6	3	2	0	4
F	G	H	I	J

The symbols have the following values:

```
÷ 7 | 6  2  5  9  1  2
      8  9  4  1  6

÷ 7 | 8  3  4  4  0
      1  1  9  2  0

  3  6        2  0        1  2
 -   3       -   8       -   2
  3  3        1  2        1  0
```

114   Both will rise.

115   A.

116   A will rise, B will drop.

117   D.

118   C. The shapes are turned onto their left side.

119   D. The star is on the wrong side in relation to the other shapes.

120   C.

121   D.

122   F. The analogy is for two items to turn 180°, without shifting their position within the set.

123   E. The values are:
bear = 5, horse = 1, fish = 4, bird = 3.
The sums are:
5 + 1 + 1 [7] = 4 + 3 [7];
3 + 3 [6] = 5 + 1 [6];
(4 − 1) [3] + 1 [4] = 3 + 1 [4].
The column is 4 + 5 + 3
[12 or fish + fish + fish].

124   A.

125   F. In all others the small ball is diagonally opposite to the two shaded spikes.

126   B. The objects are rotating one-sixth of a turn clockwise (60°) each step.

127   39 cobras.

128   B. The object flips onto its left side.

129   *see next page.*

130   14 spotted tiles.

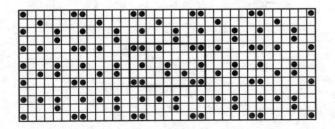

[129] C. The bicycle (worth 0) is missing.

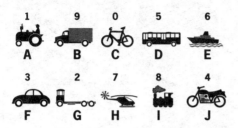

The values and working are as follows:

	1	2	6	9	3	4	25
	3	4	5	7	2	1	22
	5	7	3	4	1	8	28
	4	8	2	2	3	7	26
+	2	0	1	8	6	5	22
1	7	3	0	1	7	5	24

131 E.

132 B. The sequence of rotation is mirror-reversed.

133 A. This is a mirror-image of the other shapes' rotation.

134 C. All the others have in the middle, an enlarged version of the objects at top-left and bottom-right.

135

136 C. The internal configuration has changed hand in this shape).

137 C. The inner shapes rotate anti- (counter) clockwise; the outer shapes rotate clockwise.

138 H. The black columns of stars move to the right, as a pair, one column at a time; when a black column reaches the right edge, it returns to the left edge in the next set.

139 C. The same circles are rotated, except C, which are mirror images.

140 B.

141 C. The penguin's bill is slightly more open.

142 H.

143 C. The separate shaded cell is always one cell away from the group of three, and, if a corner group, is on the same vertical or horizontal line as the innermost cell of the group of three.

144 A.

145 17 rattlesnakes can be collected if you follow this route:

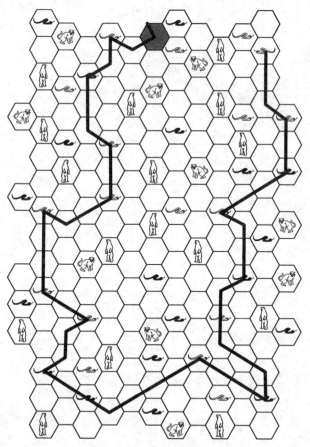

146   B. The pattern rolls to the left one step at a time.

147   The symbol is based on the number of shapes it appears in. For instance, the cone (bottom right) appears in two shapes, and the tube is in three.

148   B.

149   See next page.

150   See next page.

151   See page 214.

152   B. The balls on the diamond have switched places.

153   E. The white middle of the black flower in this set (top right) is larger than the others.

[149]

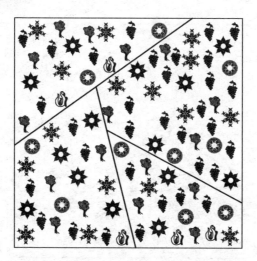

[150]

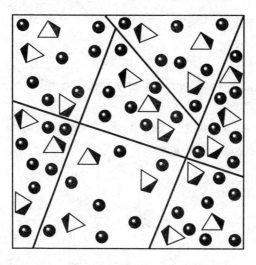

154 (a). They will reach the ground together (although they will be much further apart). As soon as the projectile is fired it is subject to gravity, and will approach the ground at the same downward speed as the brick, despite its forward motion.

[151]

155 It will rise.

156 B. The two sun symbols have reversed positions.

157 A. The lightning bolt flips upside down and changes side, as in the analogous figure.

158 B

159   G. The line shown in black is missing.

160   E. The jet fighter is rolling to the left one fifth of a turn per step.

161   B. There are only 10 circles here, but in the others there are 11.

162   E. Fire is extinguised by a fire extinguisher as dirt is removed by a vacuum cleaner.

163   C. The lightning bolt and pointer shape have changed place at the bottom.

164   It will rise.

165   A and J. The loops have been distorted with respect to the others.

166   F. The figure has no eyebrows.

167   Both will fall.

168   C.

169   A will rise, B will drop.

170   D. The others are 90° rotations of the same pattern.

171   C. The angle between the hands remains the same, but in C the minute and hour hands are reversed.

172   Follow this string:

173   D.

174   B.

175   C.

Puzzle notes

Working Out

Use this Notes page and the ones that follow it to give you space for working out, if you require it.

Puzzle notes

Puzzle notes

Puzzle notes

Puzzle notes

Puzzle notes

IF YOU'VE ENJOYED THIS BOOK, WHY NOT TRY THE OTHERS IN THIS MENSA SERIES:

Title	ISBN	Author	Price
Mensa Boost Your IQ	1 85868 308 4	Carolyn Skitt & Harold Gale	£4.99
Mensa Number Puzzles	1 85868 309 2	Harold Gale	£4.99
Mensa Riddles & Conundrums	1 85868 310 6	Robert Allen	£4.99
Mensa Word Puzzles	1 85868 311 4	Harold Gale	£4.99
Mensa Number Puzzles For Kids	1 85868 312 2	Carolyn Skitt & Harold Gale	£3.99
Mensa Mind Mazes For Kids	1 85868 313 0	Robert Allen	£3.99
Mensa Word Puzzles For Kids	1 85868 314 9	Robert Allen	£3.99
Mensa Secret Codes For Kids	1 85868 315 7	Robert Allen	£3.99
Mensa Logic Brainteasers	1 85868 545 1	Philip Carter & Ken Russell	£4.99
Mensa Mind Workout	1 85868 546 X	Josephine Fulton & Robert Allen	£4.99
Mensa Know Yourself	1 85868 547 8	Josephine Fulton	£4.99

These Mensa books and many others are available from all good bookshops, or they may be ordered by telephone from Books By Post on (01624) 675 137.